W9-BBW-091

MICRO MANIA

A Really Close-Up Look at Bacteria, Bedbugs & the Zillions of Other Gross Little Creatures That Live In, On & All Around You!

Jordan D. Brown

imagine!
New York
www.imaginebks.com

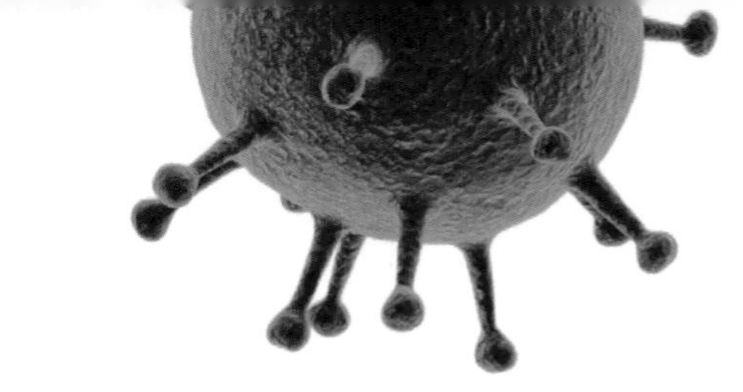
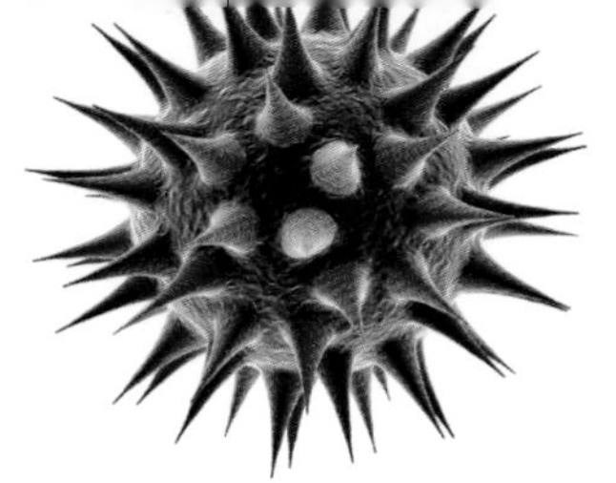
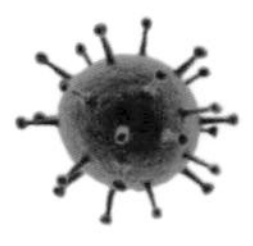

For my not-so-little ones, Finian and Olivia, who are getting bigger every day.

Published by Imagine Publishing, Inc.
25 Whitman Road, Morganville, NJ 07751

Distributed in the United States of America by
BookMasters Distribution Services, Inc.
30 Amberwood Parkway, Ashland, OH 44805

Distributed in Canada by
BookMasters Distribution Services, Inc.
c/o Jacqueline Gross Associates, 165 Dufferin Street, Toronto, Ontario, Canada M6K 3H6

Distributed in the United Kingdom by
Publishers Group UK
8 The Arena, Mollison Avenue,
Enfield, EN3 7NL, UK

ISBN-10: 0-9823064-2-3
ISBN-13: 978-0-9823064-2-0
Library of Congress Control Number: 2009922008

Designed by Marc Cheshire

Printed in China

10 9 8 7 6 5 4 3 2 1

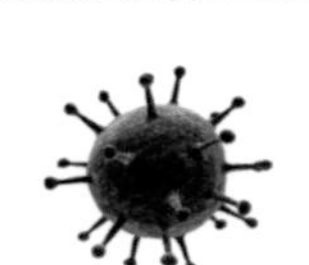

Acknowledgements: A zillion thanks to photo researcher Dawn Cusick for finding the incredible images, to designer Marc Cheshire for the dazzling designs, to copyeditor Joe Rhatigan for his keen eye, and to editor Heather Quinlan for her smart suggestions, and for always pushing me to "make it grosser."

Image credits:

Adstock: 9

Gary Albrecht: 54 (top)

BigStockPhoto: 2, 3, 4, 6, 30, 46 (middle), 47, 52, 54 (bottom), 55, 58, 59, 60, 69, and 74

Finian Harper Brown: author photo (jacket)

Centers for Disease Control and Prevention (CDC): 12 (top right) (Dr. Barry S. Fields), 15, 21 (right) (Betsy Crane), 31 (far right), and 57 (Harvard University, Dr. Gary Alpert, Dr. Harold Harlan, and Richard Pollack)

Clemson University/USDA Cooperative Extension Slide Series, Bugwood.org: 43 (top)

Dr. John D. Cunningham/Visuals Unlimited, Inc.: 62 (right)

Dr. Michael Daly: front cover (bottom row, fifth from left)

J. M. Ehrman, Digital Microscopy Facility, Mount Allison University: 79

Dennis Hlynsky: 32 (bottom)

iStockphoto: 7, 10, 11, 12 (top left), 13, 18, 19, 20, 22, 23, 24, 25, 26, 27, 28, 29, 31, 32 (top), 33, 34, 35 (top), 37, 39, 40, 41 (top), 43 (bottom), 45, 46 (top), 50, 51, 64 (center), 70, 72, 75, and 78

© Dennis Kunkel Microscopy, Inc.: 44

Dennis Kunkel Microscopy, Inc./Visuals Unlimited, Inc.: 76

Manigault Slide Collection, Department of Entomology, Soils, and Plant Sciences, Clemson University: 41 (bottom)

Joel Mills: 17

National Aeronautics and Space Administration (NASA): 66

National Museum of Health and Medicine: 8

National Oceanic & Atmospheric Administration (NOAA): 23 (right), 62 (left) (Dr. Louis M. Herman), 63 (top left, top right, bottom left, bottom right), 65 (Operation Deep Scope 2005 Expedition), 67 (Matt Wilson and Jay Clark), and page 71 (all) (Great Lakes Sea Grant Extension Office)

Daryl Reed: 68 (right)

United States Department of Agriculture (USDA): 14 (photo Sharon Franklin, colorization Stephen Ausmus), 21 (left), 35 (Scott Bauer), 36 (photo P.J. Guard-Petter, colorization Stephen Ausmus), 42 (Rob Flynn), 48 (photo Eric Erbe, colorization Chris Pooley), and 56 (photo Eric Erbe, colorization Chris Pooley)

Wim van Egmond/Visuals Unlimited, Inc.: 64 (top right)

Dr. James Wood: 68 (left)

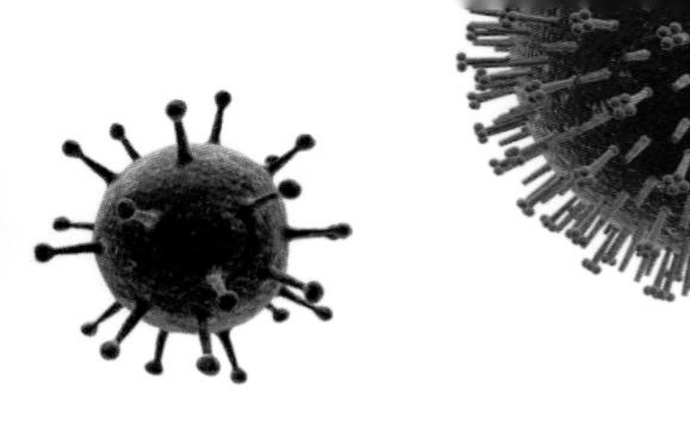
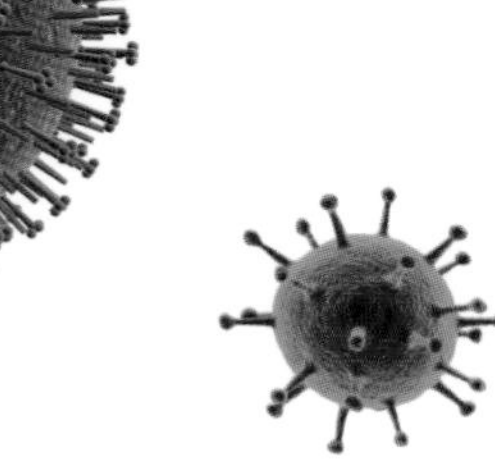

CONTENTS

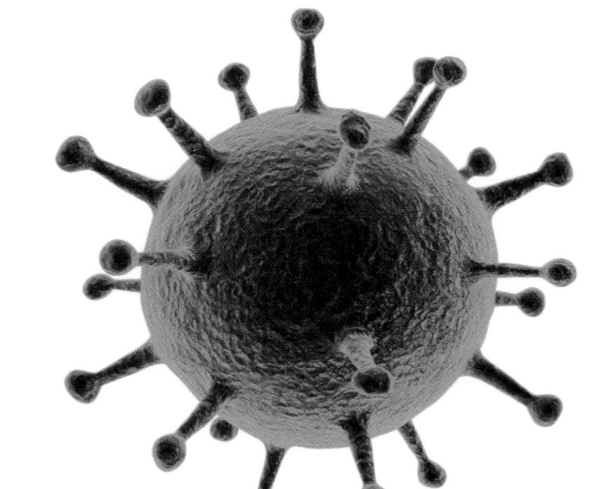

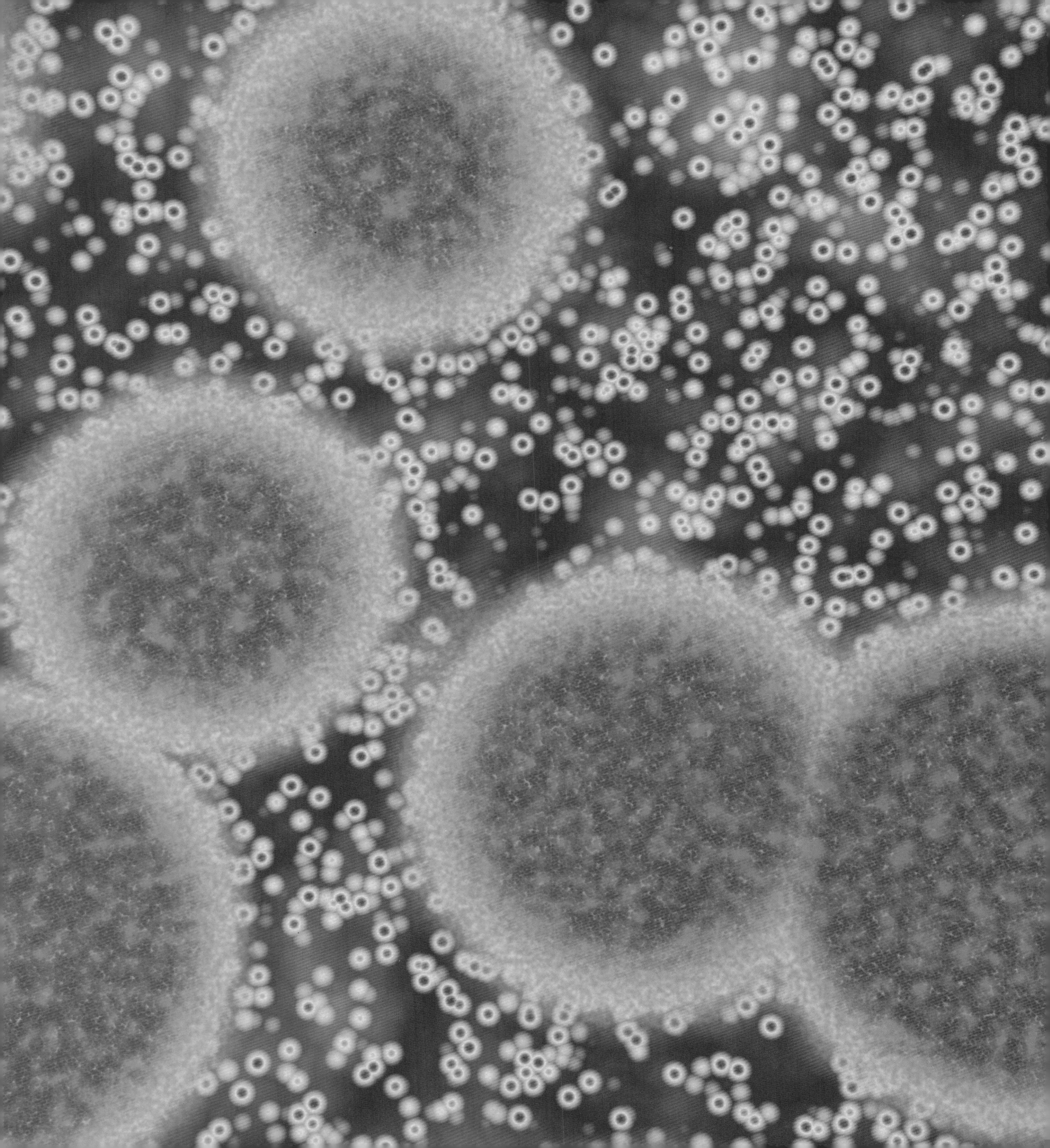

CHAPTER

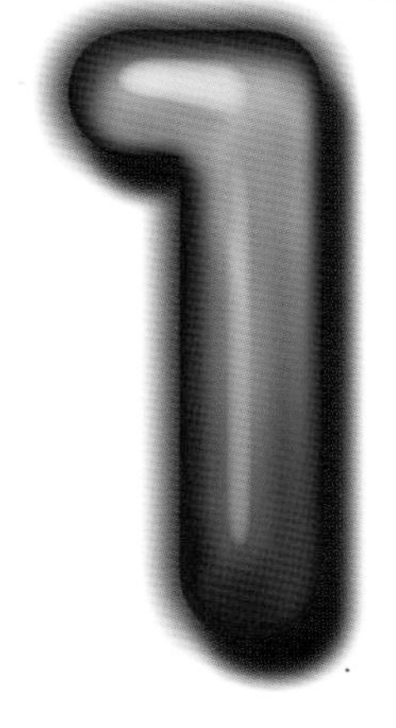

You're Never Alone

Try not to panic, but there are billions of tiny creatures crawling all over your skin. They are wriggling on your legs, your arms, your neck, your scalp . . . EVERYWHERE! And get this—these teeny critters survive by chowing down on the millions of little pieces of dead skin that you shed every day. (Hey! Quit scratching and keep reading.)

And that's just the outside of your body. Trillions more of these itty-bitty things live inside your body. Like it or not, they squirm around in your intestines, invade your nose, and cause stinky breath in your mouth. These mini-organisms—known as *bacteria*—can only be seen with a microscope. But thanks to the hard work of curious scientists, we know these little creatures can eat, breathe, move, and make more "baby bacteria" in as little as fifteen minutes.

Before you boil your body or kill the next curious scientist you see, you should know:

- Everyone's body is home to countless bacteria
- Without all these bacteria, you'd be dead.

From watching TV commercials for soap, you might think that all bacteria are bad. Sure, some kinds of bacteria, known as *germs*, can cause diseases, and even death. But most bacteria are either totally harmless or very helpful. For starters, bacteria created most of the oxygen you breathe. And remember all those bacteria living on your skin? They do a very important job. These "good bacteria" help keep you healthy by crowding out all the "bad bacteria" that would love to join the party. The bacteria that live in your gut (intestines) help keep us alive in two ways. First, they help digest our food, so our bodies can have energy and nutrients. Second, as they break down our grub, they create vitamins K and B12, which we need to survive.

OPPOSITE PAGE: *Virus cells, greatly magnified (color treated so they're easier to see)*

Some microbes are yummy! This whole-wheat bread's dough would never have risen without itty-bitty yeast fungi.

Microbes such as bacteria and yeast are needed to make some of our favorite foods, including bread, chocolate, cheese, yogurt, and more. Microbes in the air and ground also do an important clean-up job—they break down and eat dead plants and animals. Let's say, a squirrel dies in the woods. Shortly after, other animals, including insects, come by to nibble the squirrel's remains. Even if no visible scavengers chow down on its corpse, billions of microbes dine on the ex-squirrel. Thanks to billions of hungry bacteria and other microbes, it doesn't take long for a dead squirrel to go from a freshly dead body, to a mushy mess, to a pile of bones.

This little dead wasp is a hearty meal for millions of bacteria.

Microbes' ability to break down dead animal bodies is more important than you probably realize. Scientists estimate that about 110 billion humans have ever lived on Earth. (Today, there are "only" about 6.5 billion people on the planet.) If microbes had not gradually gobbled up the bodies of all the people who died, then every bit of land would be totally covered with corpses. That's right, your neighborhood would be completely littered with dead bodies.

Bacteria break down dead bodies such as these ex-fish in Salton Sea, California.

Bodies on every sidewalk, every lawn, and every parking lot! On your way to the school bus, you and your friends might have to step over a dead Revolutionary War soldier, whose body had been around since the 1700s. Imagine how different basketball games would be! Teammates might have to push bodies out of the way before making a jump shot. While this situation would be great for a horror movie, it would not be a pretty picture for the people still living. We're not even talking about the countless other animals and plants that have ever lived! In short, without bacteria breaking down all the dead bodies, the world would be a very different (and cluttered) place.

If you're still thinking, "Big deal! Who needs these microbes, anyway?" consider this: Before bacteria appeared about 3.5

billion years ago, there was no life on our planet! According to fossils, bacteria were the only living things around for millions of years. Eventually, these one-celled "earthlings" evolved slowly into every living thing on the planet today. Matt Kane of the National Science Foundation points out, "If all of Earth's microbes died, so would everything else . . . including us. But if everything else died, microbes would do just fine . . . we need microbes more than they need us."

Antony van Leeuwenhoek (1632-1723)
(Last name pronounced "LAY-ven-hook")

THE WORLD'S FIRST "MICRO MANIAC"

When most people have diarrhea, their first thought isn't, "Ooh, I wonder what this brown, runny stuff looks like really close-up!" But Anton van Leeuwenhoek wasn't like most people. He was a super curious, totally obsessed, and extremely patient man who lived in Holland about 350 years ago. Not only did he look at his diarrhea under a microscope, but he also spent his free time getting microscopic views of blood, sweat, urine, pus, puke, and more. Name any yucky fluid that oozes, gushes, or squirts out of your body, and you can bet that van Leeuwenhoek was eager to find out what made it tick (or squirm, as the case may be). Thanks to his incredible curiosity and dedication, van Leeuwenhoek made one of the world's most amazing scientific discoveries. In 1675, he became the first person ever to see microbes!

Van Leeuwenhoek didn't start off as a scientist. As a teenager, he trained to be a cloth salesman. As part of this job, van Leeuwenhoek used a magnifying glass to study fabric up close. This handy tool allowed him to make things look about three-times bigger than their real size. For fun, van Leeuwenhoek loved to use his magnifying glass to look at other things, too, like insects and fingerprints. In the 1660s, van Leeuwenhoek read a book by a famous scientist named Robert Hooke. This book, entitled *Micrographia*, had big foldout pages with detailed drawings of what different plants and animals looked

like under a microscope. Van Leeuwenhoek was fascinated by the close-up pictures of a fly's eye, a plant cell, and much more. Eager to explore the natural world for himself, van Leeuwenhoek decided to make his own microscopes. With practice and patience, he got very good at creating them. His best microscopic lenses could magnify things more than 200 times. Van Leeuwenhoek's homemade microscopes didn't look anything like the microscopes of today. They only had one lens and were more like a super powerful magnifying glass. But by holding these lenses up to the sun, he could do some strange and interesting experiments.

Van Leeuwenhoek's homemade microscope didn't look anything like the microscopes you've probably seen. In this model, you can see that van Leeuwenhoek's tool was made mostly of metal, was about three inches long, and had room for only a single glass lens. A lens is a piece of glass that has been grinded into a shape that can magnify things when held up to bright light. Over his lifetime, van Leeuwenhoek made hundreds of homemade microscopes, of which only nine survive today.

One day, for example, van Leeuwenhoek scraped white scum from his teeth and mixed it with water. When viewed under his microscope, he saw "many very little living animalcules." To learn more, he scraped the gunk off the teeth of an old

Eye-to-eye with a fly (greatly magnified, of course)

man who never brushed. What did he find? Even MORE of these tiny squirming creatures! Today we know that what van Leeuwenhoek saw were the bacteria that cause plaque in our mouths. Van Leeuwenhoek discovered that he could kill these bacteria in his mouth by drinking hot coffee.

In other experiments, van Leeuwenhoek used his microscopes to observe the hundreds of tiny creatures swimming around in a single drop of water from a lake. He made special microscopes that allowed him to watch how blood flowed in rabbits' ears and bats' wings. In addition to looking at his own diarrhea, he examined the poop of various creatures including chickens, frogs, horses, and cows. By the time he died, he had made over 500 microscopes and examined thousands of things under them. (If he could have examined his own dead body under one of his microscopes, he probably would have!)

Van Leeuwenhoek didn't do all this research for fame or

money. Instead, it was all about satisfying his curiosity, and sharing his discoveries with others. As an old man, he wrote: ". . . my work, which I've done for a long time, was not pursued in order to gain the praise I now enjoy, but chiefly from a craving after knowledge, which I notice resides in me more than in most other men."

THE WILD WORLD OF MICROBES

Imagine that your body had a special button next to your eyes. When you pressed it, your sight became magnified. The more you clicked it, the closer and closer you could look at things. If you had super vision, the world would appear quite different. You'd be able to look around a kitchen or bathroom and spot bacteria, and many other sorts of microscopic hitchhikers.

As you read this book, you'll meet many different kinds of microscopic life. Keep in mind that even though we call all these single-cell creatures "microbes," there is tremendous diversity. There are many thousands of different kinds of bacteria—most of which are harmless to us. And bacteria aren't the only "little guys" in town. The remarkable world of microbes also includes protozoa and viruses.

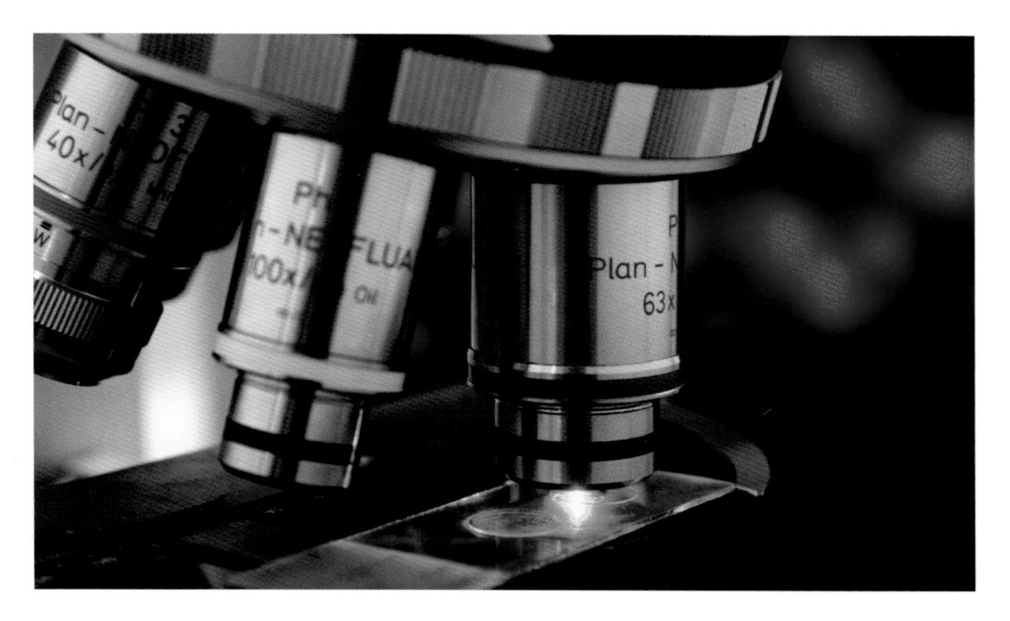

This modern microscope is much more powerful than the homemade ones van Leeuwenhoek used in the 1600s.

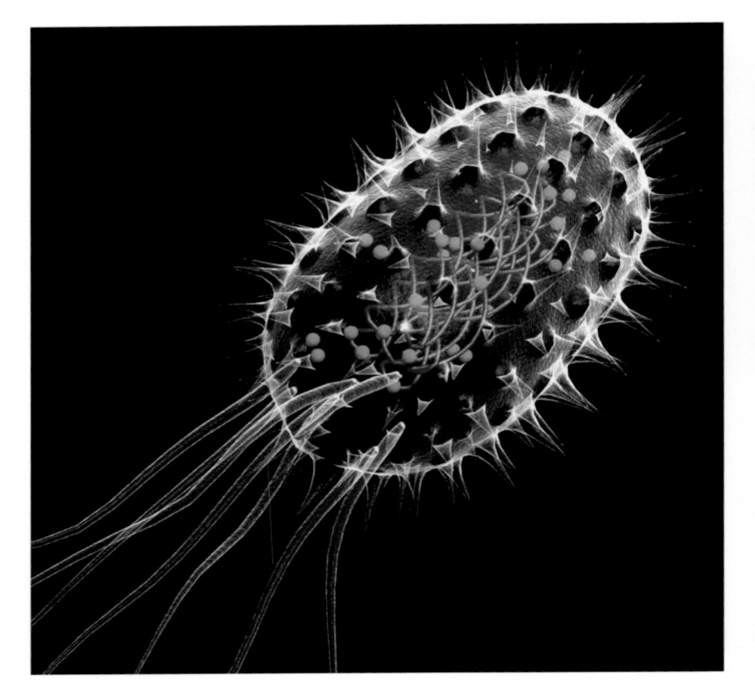

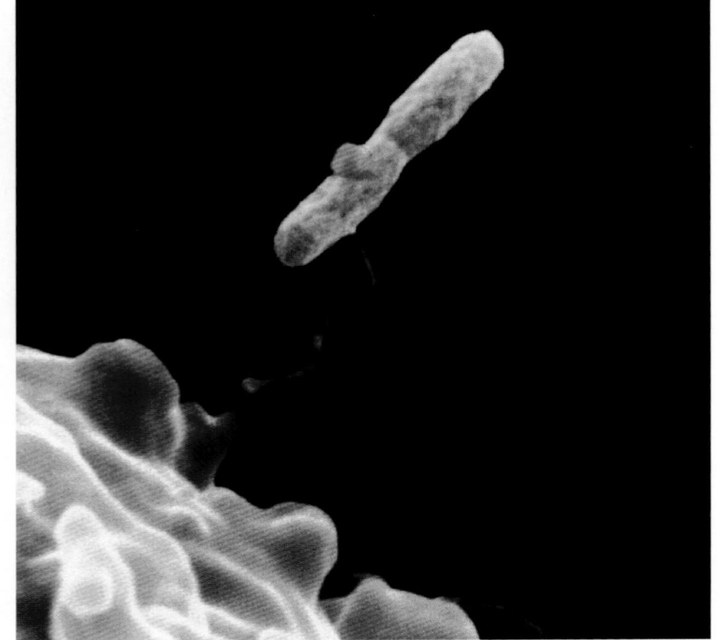

TOP LEFT: *A computer model of a bacterium on the move*
TOP RIGHT: *In this super close-up photo, a hungry amoeba (pink) uses its tail-like flagellum to grab a snack—a bacterium (green).*
OPPOSITE PAGE: *3-D, color-enhanced view of bacteria*

Facts about Bacteria

- Can be found everywhere—from the tops of the highest mountains to the bottom of the deepest oceans.
- About 10,000 species of bacteria have been described, but there are probably millions of other kinds yet to be discovered.
- They come in many different shapes including balls, rods, commas, cubes, and spirals.
- The air is full of bacteria. Every time you open your mouth, bacteria enter it. Most are killed either by enzymes in your mouth, or by the acids in your stomach when you swallow.
- Some bacteria can travel by themselves. Some swim with a tail called a *flagellum*, while they slide on slimy secretions. These little guys are *fast*. They can travel at about 50 to 60 body lengths per second. The fastest land animal, the cheetah, can run as fast as a speeding car—but it is still slower than bacteria.

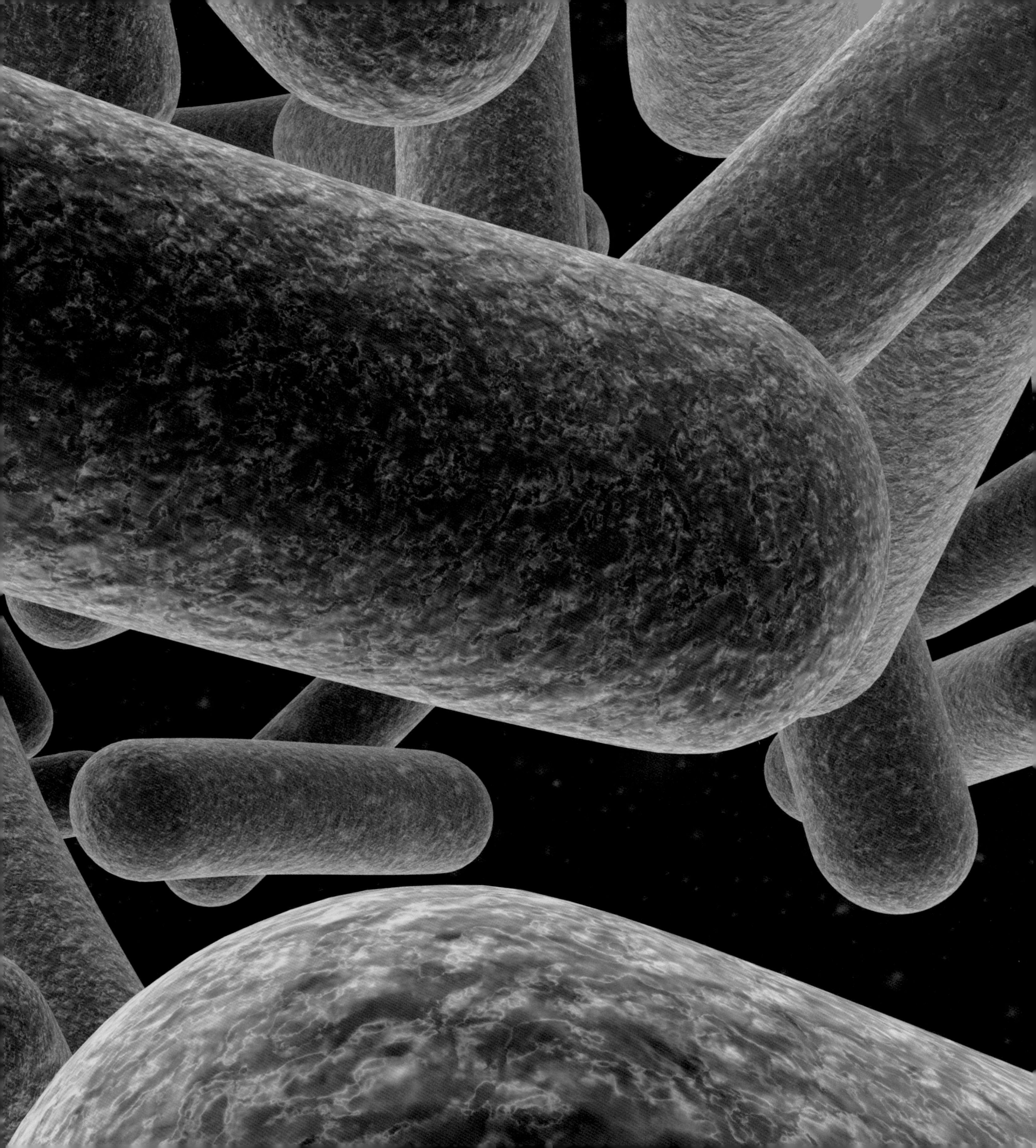

No, that's not a fingertip! It's a close-up view of an Entodinium *protozoan.*

Facts about Protozoa

- The largest kind of microbe.
- About 40,000 different kinds known, only a few cause diseases in people.
- Most protozoa live in wet environments, from moist soil to the ocean.

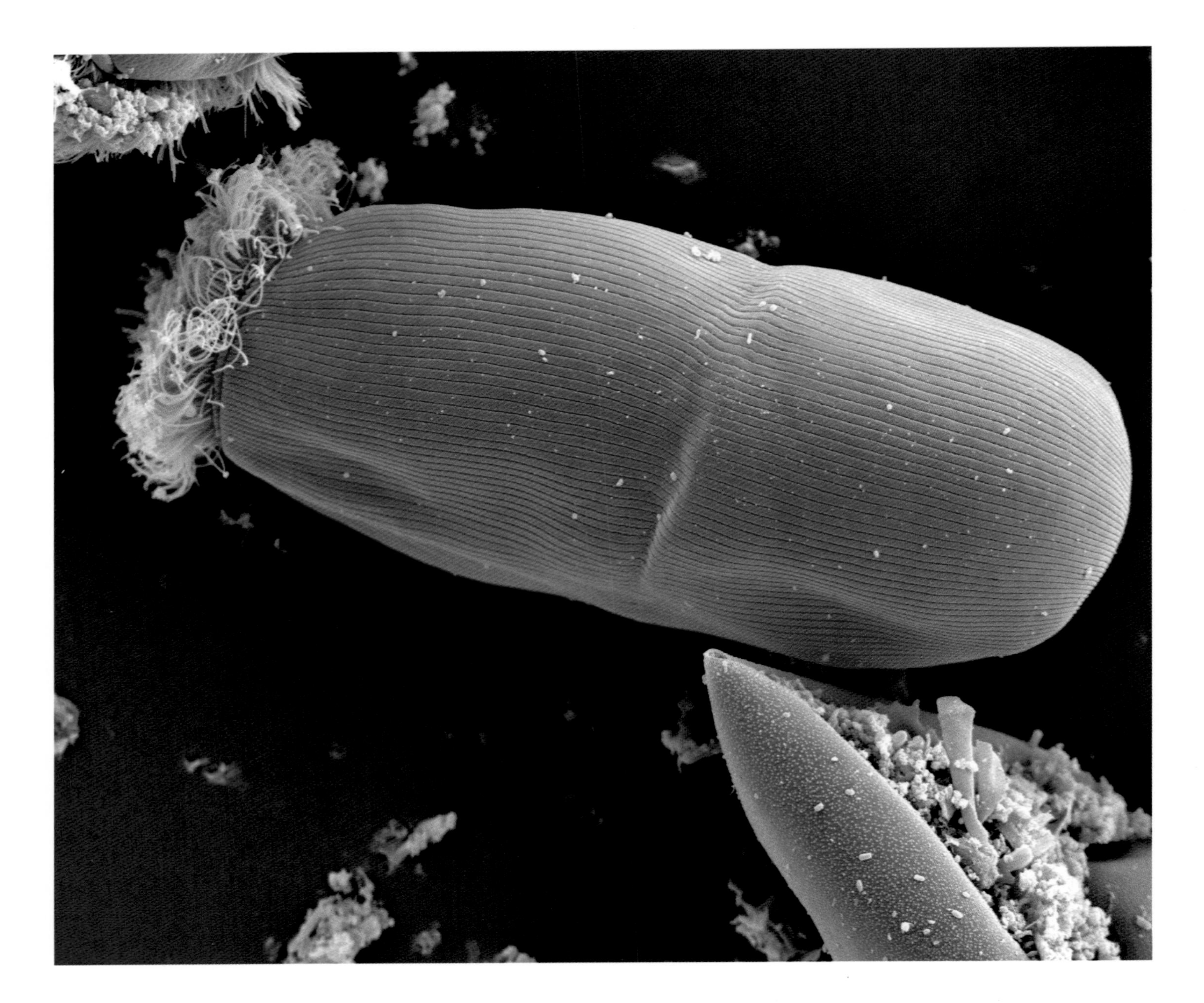

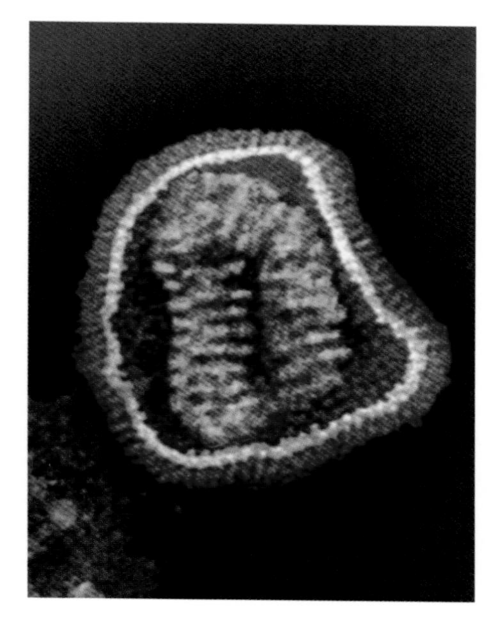

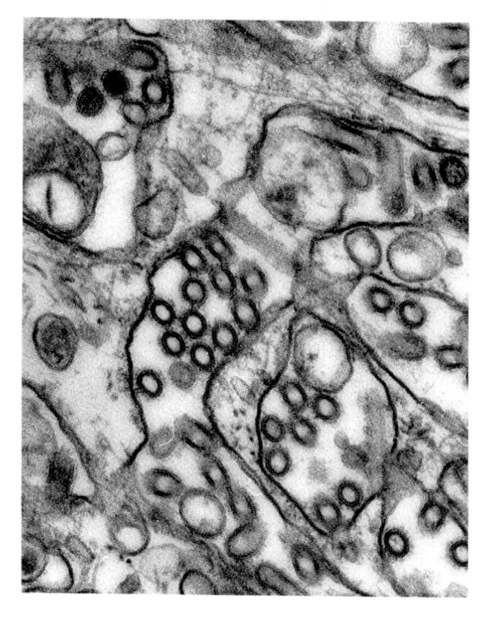

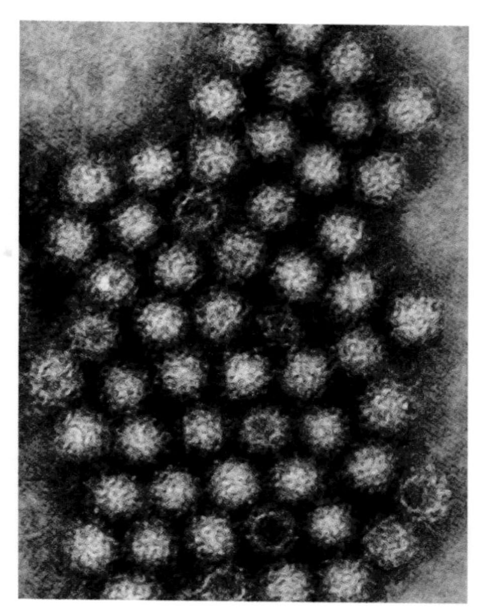

TOP LEFT: *Super close-up view of an influenza virus particle, or* virion
CENTER: *Many viruses, like the colorized Avian Influenza A virus here do not usually infect humans.*
RIGHT: *Close-up view of a norovirus, which can cause stomach flu in people*

Facts about Viruses

- Viruses are *much* smaller than the other kinds of microbes. Van Leeuwenhoek's microscopes were too weak to see viruses. To help you appreciate the size difference, if a bacterium (just one bacteria) were as large as a school bus, then a virus would only be the size of a worm. How many worms could fit inside a bus?

- The most common virus is the cold virus, of which there are 130 kinds.

- Once your body has fought a specific virus, you cannot get sick from that virus again. That's why you can only get chicken pox once. If your body has fought off one kind of cold virus, you won't get that particular cold again. But there are more than a hundred different cold viruses, so be careful of people sneezing near you.

- Viruses can mutate and change quickly to survive in different environments.

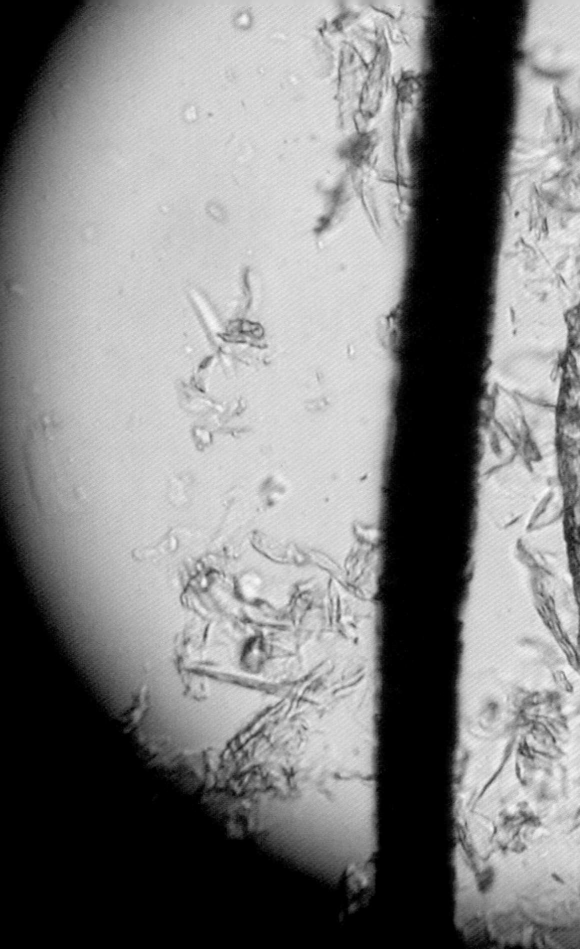
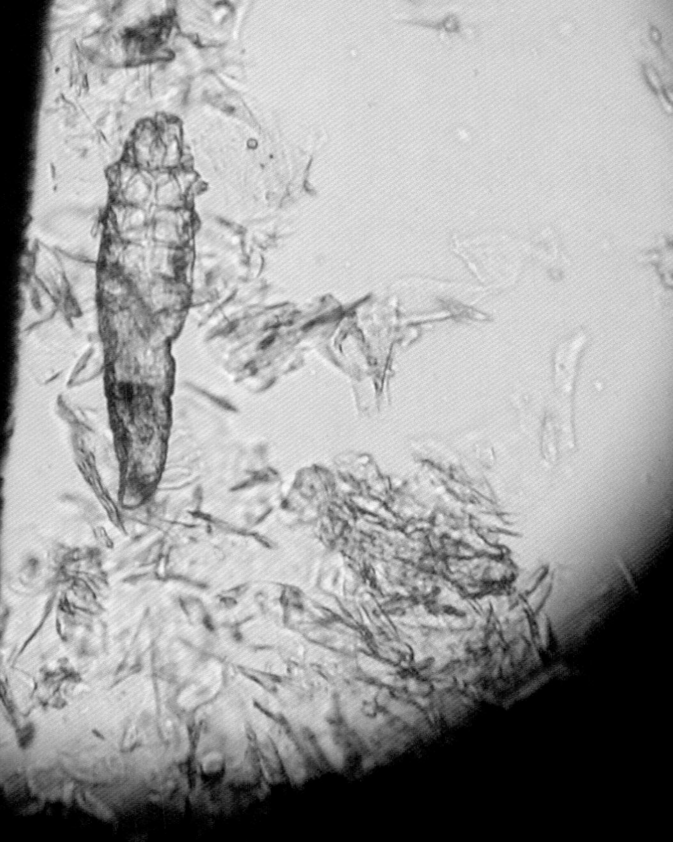

OTHER MICRO LIFE

In addition to microbes, there are many other tiny little creatures that share the world with us. *Demodex* mites, for example, are long, eight-legged animals that live in the follicles of your eyelashes. Don't worry—they are harmless! They feed on the oils and other fluids from your eye. They spend their whole lives there, except for maybe taking a "micro scroll" around your face at night. (Scratch away, they're still there . . . or under your fingernails now.)

Another kind of mites called *dust mites* hang out in our beds. The average bed has more than a million of them. They survive by eating all the dead skin cells that fall off your body when you're snoozing.

Tiny, harmless, eight-legged Demodex *mites like this one probably live on your eyelashes. This one came from a dog.*

While some of this book will focus on creatures that are too small to see without a microscope, some chapters will introduce you to barely visible animals.

WHO'S RUNNING THE SHOW?

When we think about the creatures on Earth, it is easy to believe that humans and other large animals are the most important life forms. (After all, how many microbes have game shows?) But the truth is that there are many more insects, spiders, and microbes than there are larger animals. It's really the little guys who are in charge.

The last time you went to the doctor's office for a checkup, did the nurse ask you to step on a scale to find out how much you weighed? Well, some scientists are curious about the weight of different living things. Imagine you had a scale big enough to weigh every person on Earth? How about every elephant on our planet? Okay, now imagine that you had a GIANT scale that could weigh all of Earth's microbes. Which do you think would weigh more—all the visible animals, or all the invisible creatures? If you guessed all the visible animals, you're in for a surprise. All the microscopic life on Earth weighs *more* than all the visible animals put together! Sure, each individual microbe is almost weightless, but there are so many of them. Humans live mostly on land. But microbes also thrive in all the world's oceans and can survive in the hottest and coldest environments. There are more microbes on Earth than there are known stars in the universe. So, put together, their mass (weight) is enormous. One microbiologist estimates that the total number of bacteria on Earth is five million trillion trillion—that's a five with thirty zeroes after it! And bacteria are only one group of all the teeny-tiny creatures that share our planet with us.

No doubt about it: It's a small world, after all.

CHAPTER

You and Trillions of Your Close Personal Friends

It doesn't matter if you wash your hands, brush your teeth, take daily showers, or change your underwear every day. Like it or not, your body is one big bacteria party. Billions of these microscopic guys live inside you all the time (until they are pooped out!), while billions more hang out on your skin, like invisible tourists. You can never totally get rid of these countless itty-bitty creatures. But remember, that's actually a good thing. As mentioned before, without all these bacteria helping you, you'd be dead. Most of these bacteria keep us healthy by breaking down food and fighting off harmful germs.

Every living thing—from mushrooms to moose to you—is made of super-small things called *cells*. Some creatures, such as bacteria, are made of only one cell. Your body, on the other hand, is made of about 100 trillion cells (although no one's ever counted, of course). You have skin cells, nerve cells, muscle cells, blood cells, and many more kinds. And here's the shocker: Your body is home to more bacteria cells than human cells! A LOT more. Only about 10% of the cells in your body are human. The other 90% are bacteria cells that live on or in us. According to the Howard Hughes Medical Institute of Maryland, we each have about two to five pounds of live bacteria in our bodies. Put another way, if you squished together all the bacteria cells from one adult, they could fill up a half-gallon ice cream container. (Hey! Maybe someone should invent a daring new flavor: Bacteria Fudge Ripple! Yum!)

The only time in your life when your body was bacteria free was when you were in your mother's womb. You didn't need help from bacteria because your mother gave you everything you needed to survive (food, oxygen, a way to digest food, and so on). But as soon as you were born, bacteria invaded your body. Some came in through the air you breathed, while others

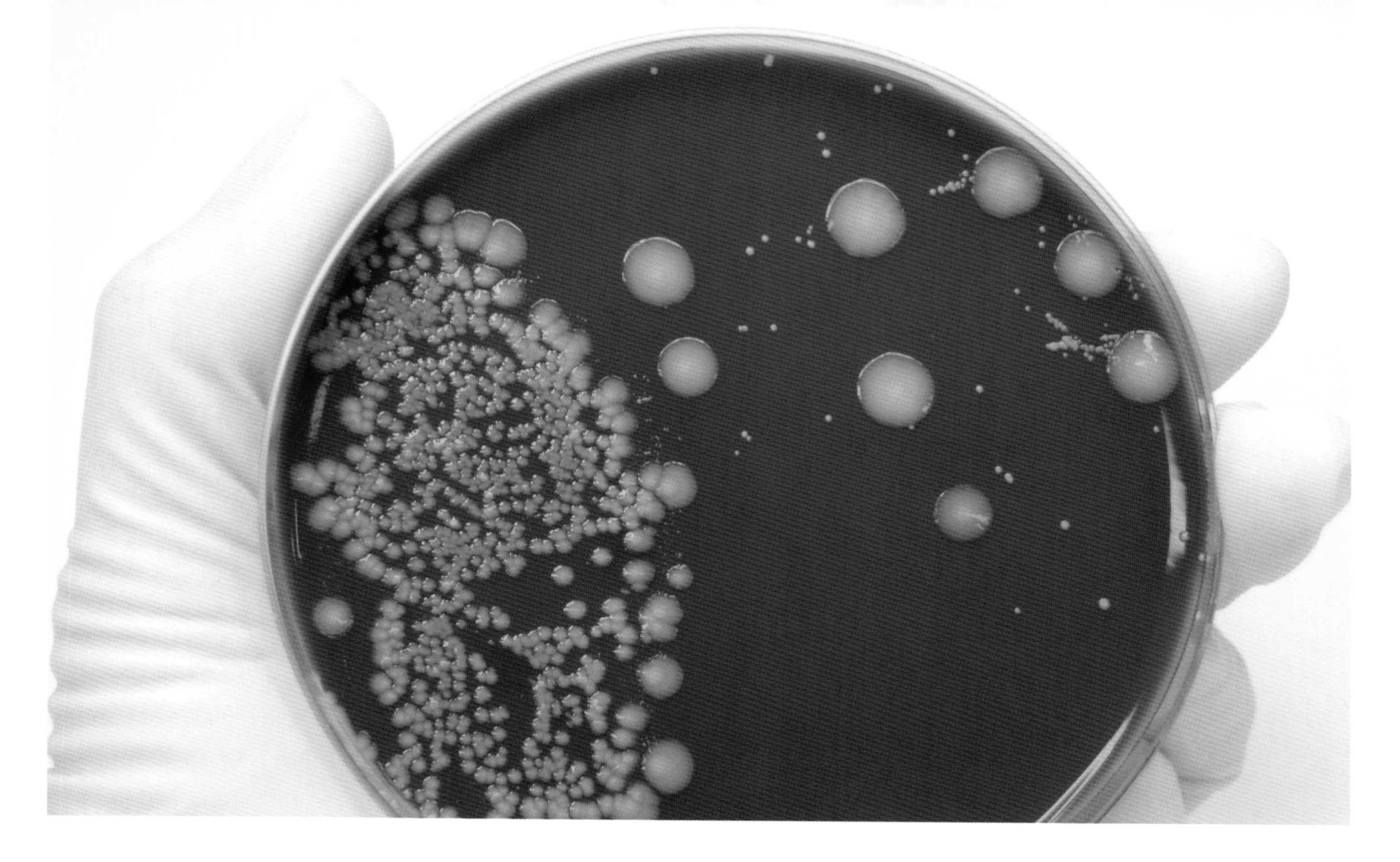

traveled inside through food and water. You know how babies love to stick their fingers in their mouth? That's another way that bacteria get in.

In this chapter, you'll meet some of the micro-aliens that live on (and in) Planet You. Since you are host to billions of bacteria and other microbes, you might as well learn more about them . . . and maybe even appreciate them.

LEFT: *Billions of bacteria already call this newborn baby "home."*
ABOVE: E. coli *bacteria growing in a petri dish (note the rubber gloves!)*

THE BEST PARTS OF YOUR BODY (ACCORDING TO BACTERIA . . .)

Some parts of your body are much more appealing to bacteria than others. In general, if a body part is dark, wet, warm, and stinky, then bacteria will thrive there. Given the choice between a dry elbow and a sweaty armpit, bacteria will go for the sweaty armpit every time. Your mouth is another place were bacteria can find the right conditions to grow like crazy. Bacteria also love to hang out and grow in your underwear, especially if

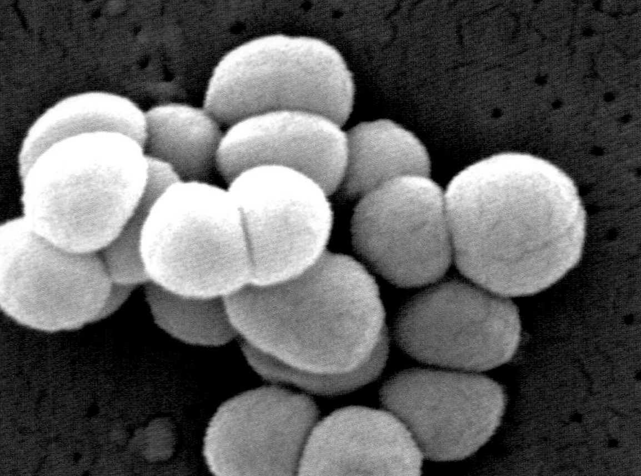

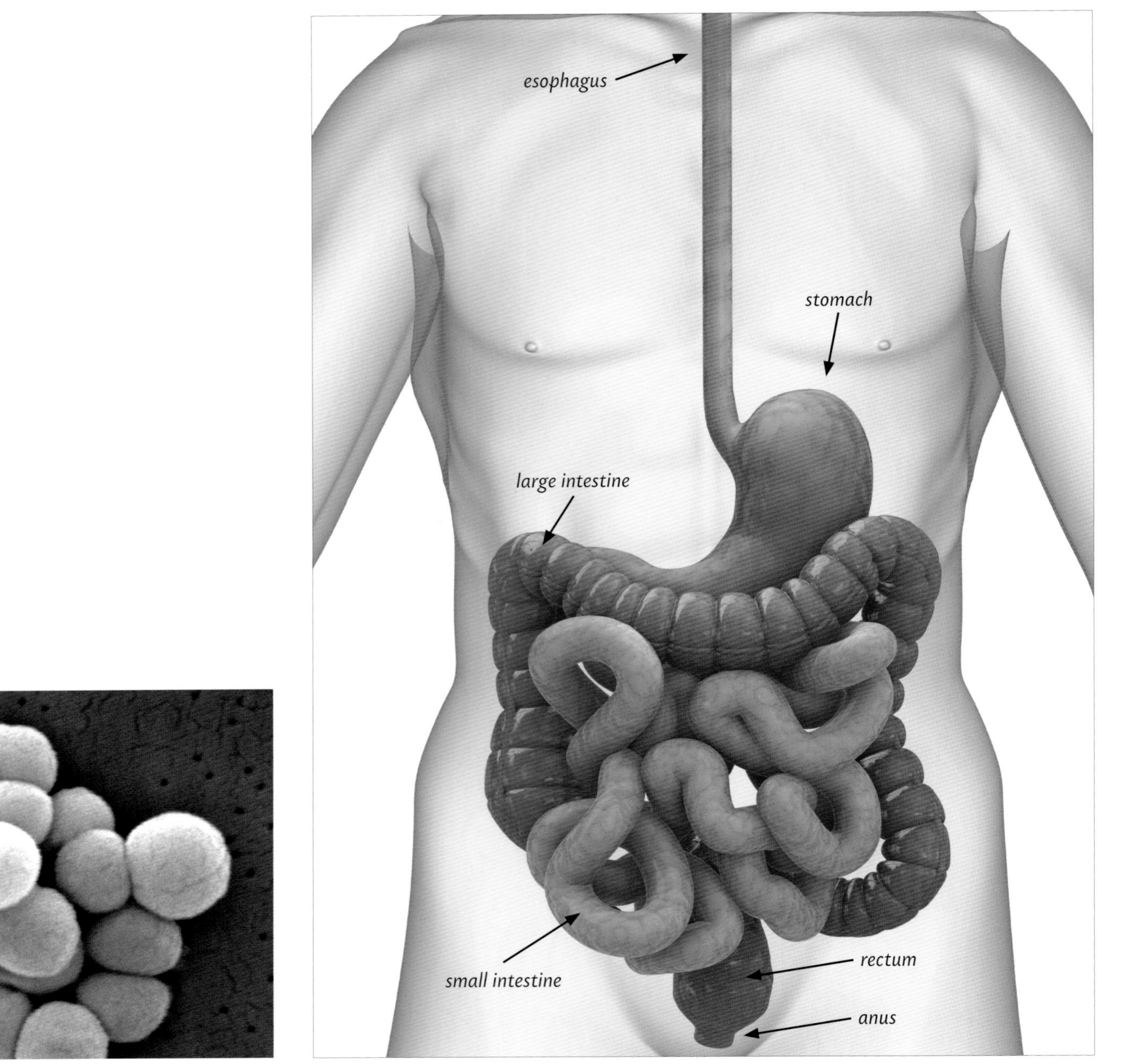

ABOVE: *A cluster of* E. coli *bacteria*
RIGHT: *The human digestive system*

you've just exercised. And it's hard to imagine a darker, wetter, warmer place than the insides of your intestines. That's why your colon is Bacteria City for your body.

Before we take a tour of the bacteria in the body, let's go over a few basic things about these hearty life forms.

Are All Bacteria the Same?

To say that all bacteria are alike is like saying all kids are the same. Are you exactly like the kids you go to school with? Sure, there are some similarities. For example, you're all human, about the same age, and share some of the same interests, such as sports, reading, or video games. But there are also many, many differences. Kids have different heights, hair colors, hobbies, tastes in food, and much more.

As for bacteria, what they have in common is the number of cells they have: one. And they're all too small to see without a microscope. (Thousands of bacteria could fit on the period at the end of this sentence.) Another similarity is that they all need food to survive. In just a bit, we'll get into what bacteria like to eat.

But in many ways, bacteria are quite different. For one thing, bacteria come in different shapes. A bacterium might look like a short hotdog, a round ball, or a spiral. Some bacteria stick together in long strings, while others float along by themselves.

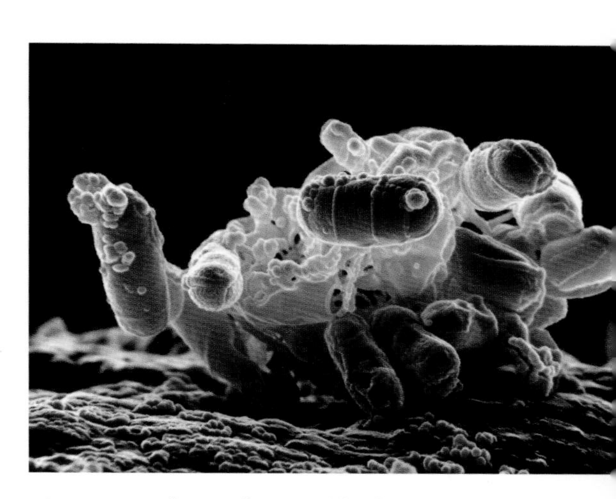

Micrococcus luteus *bacteria like these are normally found in the human mouth, and are usually harmless.*

How Do They Eat?

Just like you, bacteria need to eat to survive. But they can't cook. Hey, they don't even have mouths to munch their grub. Instead, the way they get food inside them is by gathering it from their environment. Their bodies make special chemicals called *enzymes*, which they push out through their cell wall. These enzymes break down any nearby food into tiny bits that flow back into the cell. Some bacteria can produce many kinds of enzymes, so they can eat a whole bunch of different foods. Bacteria aren't picky eaters. While some kids insist on eating only things like mac & cheese or chicken nuggets, bacteria gobble up anything they can get their enzymes on. A bacteria all-you-can-eat buffet might include spilled sugar, dead skin cells, leftover cauliflower, rotten eggs . . . you name it.

How Do They Move?

Some bacteria push themselves forward through liquids by spinning around their whip-like tails called *flagella*. Scientists have even seen bacteria reversing the direction of their flagella, so they can "swim" around in the same space. (No fancy backstrokes, though.) Other kinds of bacteria make their own thick slime so they can slide on it. (Wheeee!) Still others stick out tiny, rigid, spikes called *fimbriae* to help them grab onto surfaces. As you may know, birds and whales are able to detect Earth's magnetic field (the thing that makes a compass needle point north). But you'd probably be surprised to learn that some bacteria can do this trick, too. These floating bacteria are able to navigate by using these same magnetic fields.

How Do They Reproduce?

Many bacteria species make "baby bacteria" by a process called *fission*. During fission, a bacterium cell gradually splits into two *daughter cells*, each of which has the same shape and *DNA*. DNA is the chemical code that makes every living creature unique, and helps it pass along its genes to their children and

Freaky Fact

How long would it take just one bacterium to use fission to become one billion bacteria? If the conditions were perfect (and they rarely are), one bacterium could grow into one billion bacteria in only ten hours!

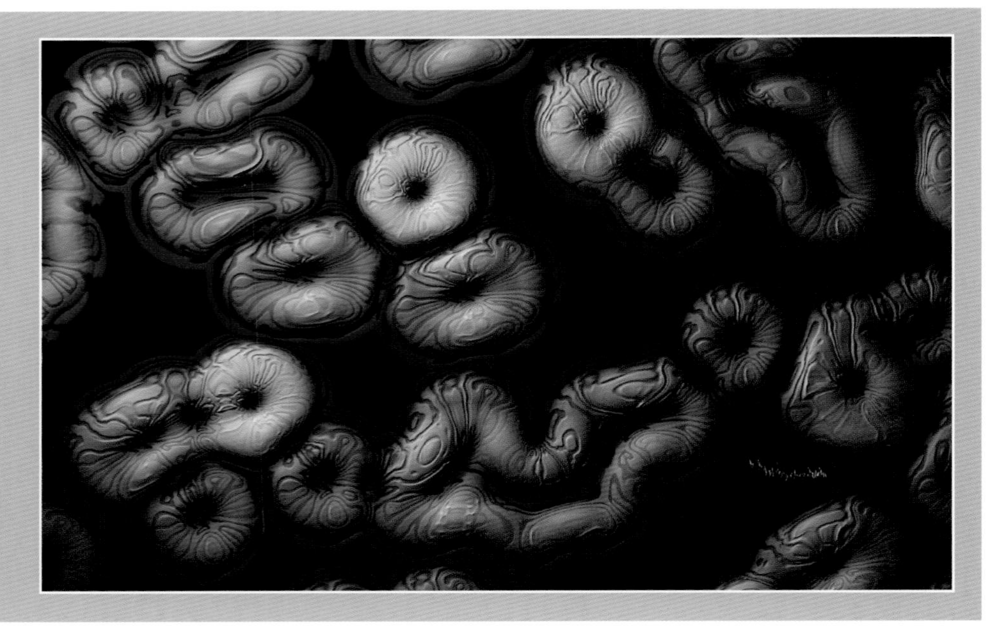

What bacteria cells dividing might look like through a powerful microscope (digitally created image)

Prochlorococcus *bacteria*

A Breath of Fresh Air

As you probably know, we all need to breathe oxygen to survive. What you probably didn't know is that at least 20% of our planet's oxygen comes from a tiny bacterium found in the world's oceans called *Prochlorococcus*. The trillions and trillions of this bacterium on our planet make their own energy through a complicated process called *photosynthesis*. Basically, plants contain a chemical called *chlorophyll* that helps them convert water, light, and carbon dioxide gas into a food source. In a happy coincidence for us, the "leftovers" of photosynthesis are gobs and gobs of oxygen.

grandchildren. By the time fission is complete, each of the daughter cells might be as large as the mother cell was before it began to split. This process doesn't take long. Some bacteria can divide about every fifteen minutes. And since each of the daughter cells also divide, in no time at all, a large bacterial population can grow. But the bacteria "kids" don't necessarily leave home right away. Some daughter cells hang together for a while, forming long, flexible chains.

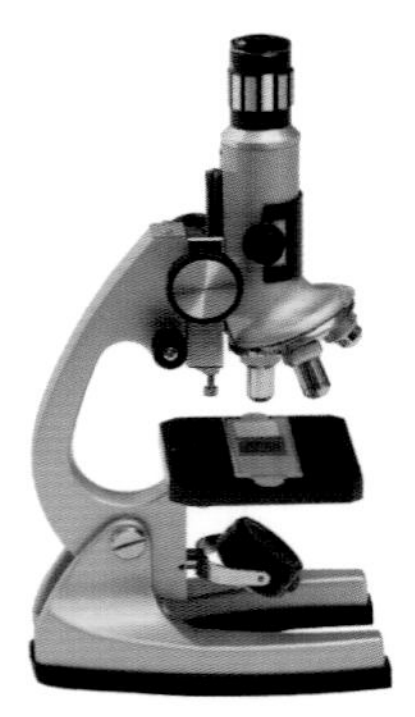

Tip: If you want to see some bacteria for yourself, a toy microscope won't help because its lenses are too weak. But if you ask a doctor or science teacher in your area if they would allow you a peek in one of their microscopes, you might get lucky!

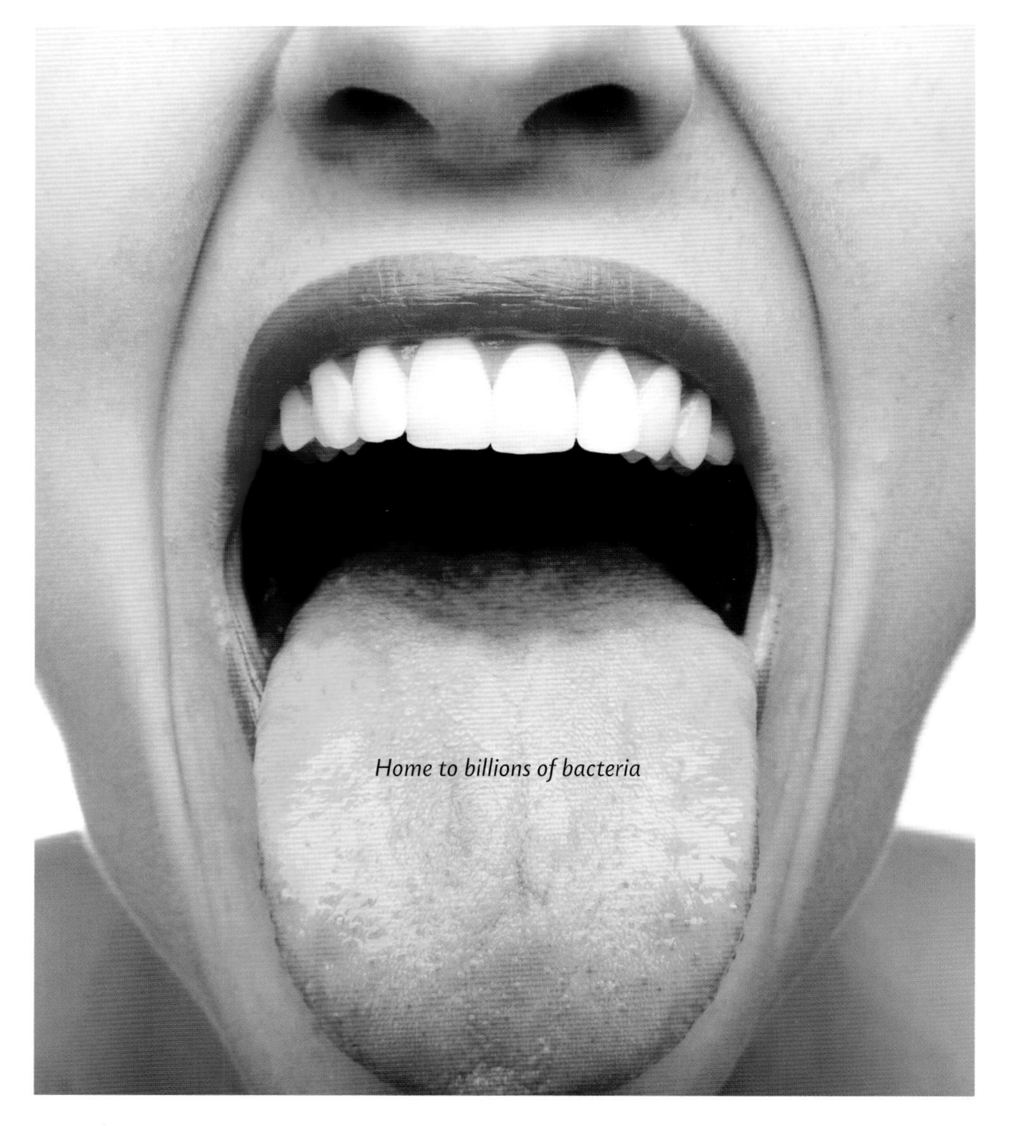

A MICROBIAL TOUR OF THE BODY

When your parents urge you to brush your teeth, don't ignore them! Because every time you take a breath, millions of bacteria enter. In fact, your mouth is home to over 500 kinds of bacteria. And the less you brush, the more you allow these microbes to grow and reproduce. And just like with your stinky feet, all those bacteria will give you stinky breath.

Even if you don't brush regularly, your saliva helps kill a bunch of these mouth bacteria by washing them into your stomach.

But not brushing can cause some harmful bacteria to survive and grow. A type of bacteria called *Streptococcus mutans* is a big fan of sugar. When you eat a big gooey piece of candy, this bacterium turns all this sugar into acids that can eat away at your teeth.

Most of the time, bad breath happens when bacteria enjoy the leftovers stuck between your teeth and on your tongue. When bacteria break down sugars and other micro-food, they release sulfur gases that we find as lovely as the smell of rotten eggs. Why does your breath usually smell especially yucky in the morning? Part of the reason is that when we sleep, our saliva flows much more slowly. When we're asleep, less saliva means that more bacteria can grow. And more bacteria equals more bad breath.

DON'T RUSH WHEN YOU BRUSH. When you brush your teeth, take your time. Get into the spaces between teeth, and remember to also brush your tongue. While this might tickle, it's a smart way to protect your mouth. Many of the bacteria found in the mouth live on the tongue.

Farty Fun Facts!

- EEEWW! Each bacterium is almost weightless, but put a bunch of them together, and it adds up. Human adults poop out their own weight in bacteria every year!
- Fart smells usually take a few seconds before they reach any nearby nostrils. Imagine if a fart could travel at the speed of sound. If so, we would be able to smell our farts at the same time we heard them.
- If someone tells you they never fart, they're lying. The average person farts about fifteen times a day.
- Some people fart shortly after they die!

Micro Life All Over Your Biggest Organ

Bacteria love warm, sweaty places. That's why each square centimeter of your biggest organ—your skin—is home to about 100,000 bacteria. Did you know that if you stretched out all the skin of a grown-up man it would cover about 2 square yards (1.7 square meters) and weigh about 9 pounds (4 kilograms)?

Sweat doesn't really have an odor. But the bacteria that dine on that sweat produce stinky smells. After they eat your sweat, bacteria release a gas that smells bad to us. (Yes, in a sense, bacteria are micro-farters!) Since the average foot has more than 250,000 sweat glands on it, it can produce a *pint* of sweat a day. Quite a smorgasbord for hungry bacteria! But if you clean the sweat off, then bacteria have nothing to eat.

TRY THIS!
The Scrubbing Challenge

Unless your hands are covered with dirt, barf, or blood, you may not feel the need to wash them . . . or wash them for more than a few seconds. But keep in mind that there are lots of invisible living things (germs) that "love" your hands so much they'll stick around and grow—unless you wash them off.

In this fun, messy experiment, we're going to pretend that tiny bits of cinnamon are harmful bacteria that would love to stick around (literally) on your hands. Your challenge is to try to get these germs off using a number of different methods.

What You Need

- small bowl
- vegetable oil
- cinnamon
- warm and cold water
- soap
- a friend or grown-up to help, if possible

What to Do

1. Pour about a cup of vegetable oil in a bowl and add about 2 tablespoons of cinnamon. Mix well.
2. Rub this cinnamon-oil mixture all over your hands.
3. Try washing your hands with just cold water for 10 seconds. What happened? How clean are your hands?
4. Put more cinnamon-oil all over your hands.
5. Try washing your hands with warm water for 30 seconds. What happened? How clean are your hands now?
6. Put more cinnamon-oil on your hands.
7. Try washing your hands with warm water and soap for 30 seconds. What happened? How clean are your hands now?

Some "Handy" Handwashing Tips

Here are some suggestions for keeping your hands and body as germ-free as possible:

When: Wash your hands every time before you eat and after you use the bathroom—especially when there's poop involved. It is also a good idea to wash up after you touch pets, blow your nose, cough, or spend time with a sick relative or friend.

How: Lather up on both sides of your hands and around your nails (where germs love to hide). Don't forget soap. Don't rush. Wash for about 30 seconds. That's about as long as it takes to sing "Happy Birthday" slowly . . . twice. (Or pick another favorite song that lasts about half a minute.) Rinse off and dry with a clean towel.

Now That Takes Guts!

The human large intestine is like Disney World for bacteria. It is dark, long (about 5 feet), and filled with bits of tasty food. (Well, the bacteria think it's tasty.) So, the entire large intestine is lined with trillions of bacteria. At least 500 species of bacteria live in our gut.

Without these helpful microbes, our bodies could not digest food. These bacteria work with other chemicals in your body to break down food and help your intestines absorb its nutrients into your body. But the bacteria don't stick around. When digested food moves through your large intestine, countless bacteria jump aboard. What you poop out (feces) is made up of about 60% bacteria.

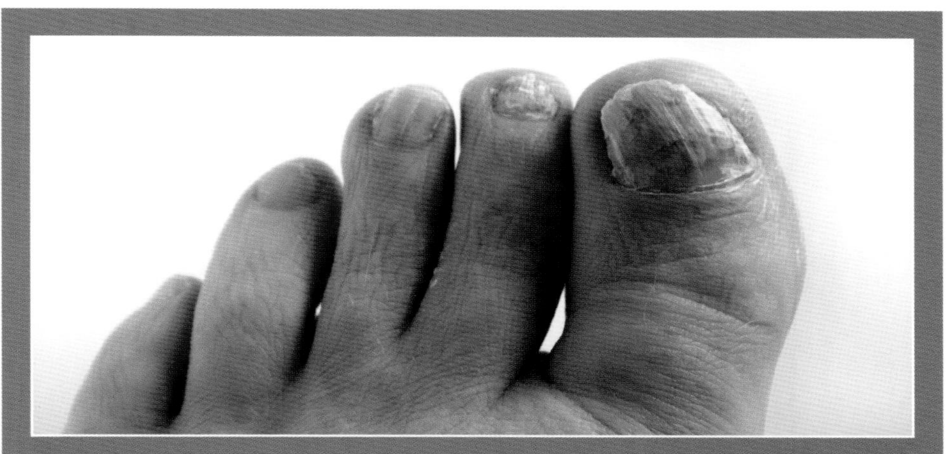

A fungus-infected foot (Onychomycosis)

Eeew! Foot Fungus!

Another kind of microbe called a *fungus* thrives in warm, dark, humid places—like the human foot. It particularly grows in-between toes, under toenails, and on the side and bottom of the foot. This fungus sometimes spreads from person to person in warm, wet places such as public showers, pools, and locker rooms (hence the nickname for this condition: *athlete's foot*). The good news is that this type of fungus can be easily treated by special anti-fungal creams, shampoos, and pills that you can get from a doctor. Another way to prevent the growth of fungi on your feet is to keep your feet clean and change your socks at least once a day.

CHAPTER 3

Pets and Pests

If you could have any pet in the world, what would you pick? A dog or a cat? Maybe a cute little bunny or a curious turtle? Whatever animal you pick, there's a good chance that many teeny-tiny creatures would love your pet as much as you. The only difference would be that instead of living with your pet, these little critters would live on or in it. In this chapter, you'll meet some tiny blood-sucking bugs like fleas and ticks, which you can see if you squint. You'll also get a close-up look at some super-small creatures called *Salmonella* bacteria that can only be viewed with a powerful microscope.

UP, UP, AND AWAY!

Some dogs are amazing jumpers. In October 2006, for example, a greyhound set the world record by leaping more than six feet into the air. Impressive, right? But some insects that love to live on dogs are even more powerful jumpers. Fleas, for example, are among the Olympic gymnasts of the bug world. A flea the size of a chocolate sprinkle can jump up more than a foot into the air. If you had that kind of jumping power, you could leap over a skyscraper!

BLOOD-SUCKING BUGS

Why do fleas need to jump so high? To reach their favorite meal, of course—blood! Fleas don't have wings, so they need powerful legs to jump high enough to get onboard the nearest animal. Fleas are *parasites*, a type of animal that survives by feeding on the blood of other animals called *hosts*. Fleas are fond of furry creatures and frequently live on dogs, cats, rats, squirrels—and humans! Some types of fleas can only live on a certain animal, while other species aren't that picky. They get their blood anywhere they can find it. (Even though scientists call the dog or cat with fleas a host, it is unlikely that the pet is excited about throwing a party for these pests.)

Fleas don't just nibble—they gorge! For a hungry flea, a host's body is like an all-you-can-eat blood buffet! A female flea can suck up to fifteen times its body weight in blood every day. Why so much? One reason is that without all this blood, a flea would die in a few days. Another reason is that the blood gives it the energy it needs to lay lots of eggs. A mother flea usually lays a batch of about twenty to twenty-five eggs every day. In just a

Fast Flea Facts!

- The flea's flat body makes it easy for it to wiggle and crawl through the hair and feathers of their host's body. The flea's body is covered with a lot of little hairs and spikes that face backward, which makes it easy to travel across a host's body.
- BOOOOOINNNG! For their size, fleas are the best jumpers in the animal kingdom, even out-jumping frogs, grasshoppers, and kangaroos!

Jumpin' Froghoppers!

Fleas were once thought of as the best jumpers of the insect world. But scientists recently discovered that another kind of bug actually has more powerful legs. The froghopper, an itty-bitty beetle about the size of a chocolate chip (approximately 6 millimeters long), can spring more than 2 feet into the air! A flea can jump as high, but it weighs much, much less (about sixty times less) than the froghopper. Imagine trying to jump in the air while carrying a bunch of bowling balls. Not easy! Malcolm Burrows, a scientist who used high-speed video cameras to measure a froghopper's leap, pointed out: "A froghopper can exert more than 400 times its body weight; a flea can do 135 times its body weight; a grasshopper can do about eight times; and we can do about two to three times our body weight." Another group of scientists in France recently discovered that dog fleas are better jumpers than the kind that live on cats. But the cat fleas shouldn't feel too bad about this defeat. Even the best basketball player in the NBA can't jump as well as even the average flea.

Microscopic image of a dog flea (Do you think this flea has dogs?)

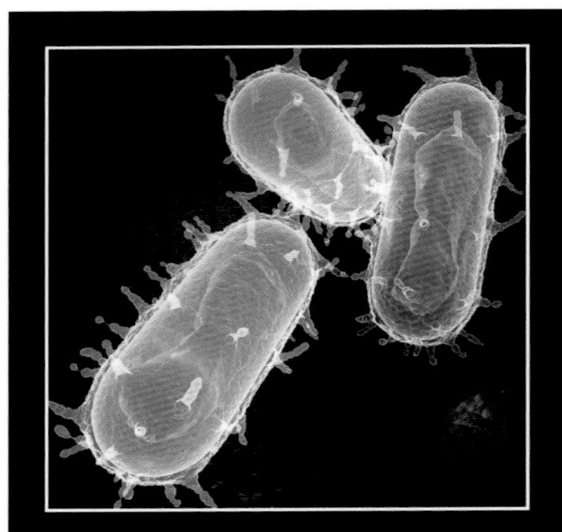

Black Death

Fleas are not only annoying to pets and their human pals. They can also spread serious diseases. In the 1300s and 1400s in Europe and Asia, during a horrible pandemic known as the Black Death, an estimated 75 million people died. The cause was a kind of bacteria known as *Yersinia pestis*, that traveled inside fleas that lived on the fur of rats. When these sneaky bacteria enter the bloodstream through a fleabite, they can go undetected by the immune system. By the time a person's body tries to fight back, it's often too late. Fortunately, this type of disease is not common today and can be treated with antibiotics.

ABOVE: *3D representation of the* Yersinia pestis *bacteria, better known as the* bubonic plague. *Carried by the fleas on rats, this infectious disease was known as the Black Death in the 1300s, and killed thousands of people a day.*

month, ten mother fleas can produce over a million kids. And of course thousands of those baby fleas will lay eggs of their own in a short time. It's easy to see how a small flea problem can grow into a big fleas problem very quickly. Furthermore, since fleas aren't that picky about their hosts, a dog with fleas might spread them to other pets in the home. And, yes, even to you! This can become a serious problem because fleas can carry diseases and little creatures called tapeworms (*Dipylidium caninum*). If a dog or small child eats a flea that is carrying tapeworm eggs, then a tapeworm can grow inside their bodies. People who have tapeworms may see tiny pieces of tapeworm in their poop that look like grains of rice. Fortunately, doctors and veterinarians can give people and pets medication to get rid of the tapeworms.

Needless to say, a home with fleas is not a fun place to live. And sometimes getting rid of them is worse—people who specialize in destroying pests, called *exterminators*, will usually have to spray your home with toxic fumes many times to make sure all the fleas and their eggs are gone.

The Fleas You Can't See

If a dog owner notices a few fleas on his pet, you might suggest, "Just give the pooch a bath and everything will be okay." Nice try! While regular baths are a good idea for a dog, it won't solve a flea problem. Why? Because most of the flea population isn't even on the dog! More than 95% of the fleas are still babies, hiding under cushions, in rugs, under furniture, and even in cracks in the floor. Basically, anywhere a furry pet likes to hang out is a likely place for baby fleas.

To grow up from freshly laid egg to blood-sucking grownup can take as little as a few weeks. During this time, fleas go through four stages, just like a butterfly: eggs, larvae, pupae, and adult.

A flea's life starts when a mother flea lays a batch of about twenty eggs. Most of these eggs will roll on the ground near where the pet sleeps. Anywhere between two days and two weeks later, the eggs hatch, and these young fleas, known as larvae, greet the world. And they're starving! These "flea kids" are blind, but they have no trouble finding something to eat. They're not picky. They'll chow down on pretty yucky things, including bits of dead skin and the poop of other adult fleas.

A larva (that's one larvae) can survive this way for several months (assuming no one vacuums the rug!). As they grow, well-fed flea larvae shed their exoskeletons three times over the course of one to two weeks. Then it's cocoon time! Yes—cocoons. Caterpillars aren't the only insects that spin them. And fleas will even build theirs from tiny fibers in your rug. Flea cocoons might not look like the ones that caterpillars spin, but the reason for spinning it is the same—to protect the insects while they're developing. A flea will develop inside for another week or so. Once inside the cocoon, the flea is called a pupa. A pupa stays inside the cocoon until it gets some clues that a host is nearby. Adult fleas don't have great eyesight—but they have other ways to find out if a furry friend is nearby.

Let's say a dog excitedly darts into a living room, barking and panting. The pupa can immediately detect the sounds and feel the vibrations. And get this—flea pupae can even sense the carbon dioxide gas that the dog

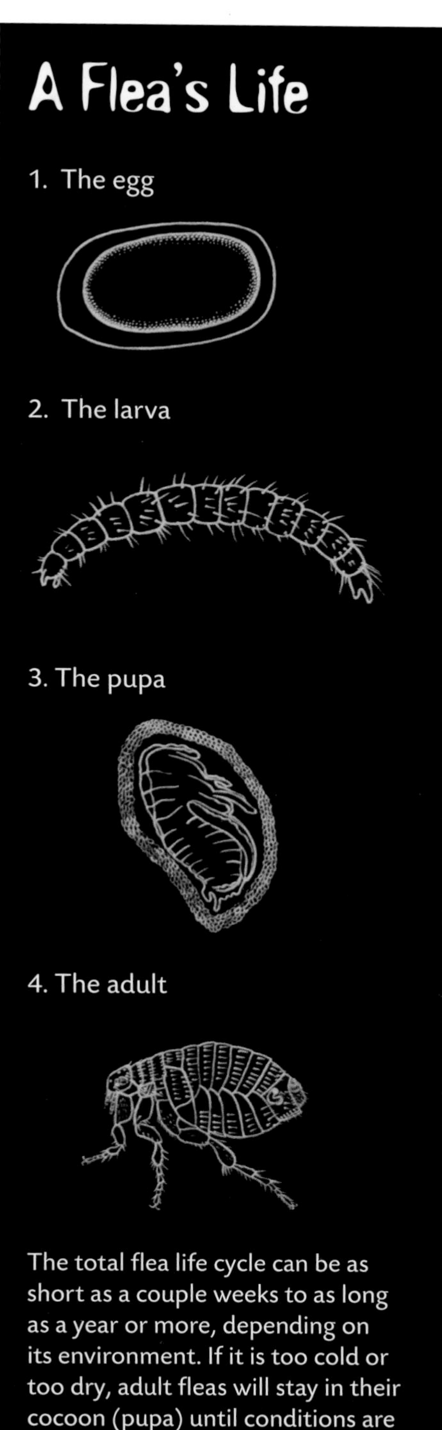

A Flea's Life

1. The egg
2. The larva
3. The pupa
4. The adult

The total flea life cycle can be as short as a couple weeks to as long as a year or more, depending on its environment. If it is too cold or too dry, adult fleas will stay in their cocoon (pupa) until conditions are right for survival.

is breathing out. If a pupa picks up on these signs, it will bust out if its cocoon and use its powerful legs to jump up on the dog's furry body. The fleas are so tiny, the dog may not even notice at first. But eventually the poor pooch will be crawling with little "pets" of its own. If, by some chance, there are no hosts nearby, flea pupae are lucky. They can survive inside their cocoon for up to a year without feeding.

A flea's buggy body may look easy to squish, but it isn't. This insect's outer layer (the *exoskeleton*) is so hard that if you squeeze it between your fingers, it probably won't die. That's why pet owners are often told by experts to kill fleas by flushing them down the toilet, burning them, or (if you're daring) crushing them between two fingernails.

Microscopic image of a dog flea. This blood-sucking insect can also feed on humans.

The Big Top for the Little Guys

In the 1800s and early 1900s, one of the most popular sideshow attractions was the flea circus. The people running these shows tried to make visitors believe that they had trained their fleas to use their strength to pulls little carts, go on small trapezes, and more. A modern circus performer named A.G. Gertsacov has created the real deal. His popular show features two performing fleas named Midge and Madge, who are invisible to the human eye, but can ride on little chariots, balance on a tiny tightrope, and fly through a small flaming hoop when shot out of a cannon. Gertsacov uses tweezers and a high-powered microscope to urge his little stars to do their mini-feats. He says his stars prefer human and pig blood, so he pricks his finger and gives them drops of blood every week or so. He uses the human flea (*Pulex irritans*) because it lives much longer than dog or cat fleas.

"Professor" A.G. Gertsacov, ringmaster and creator of the Acme Miniature Circus, examines one of his little stars.

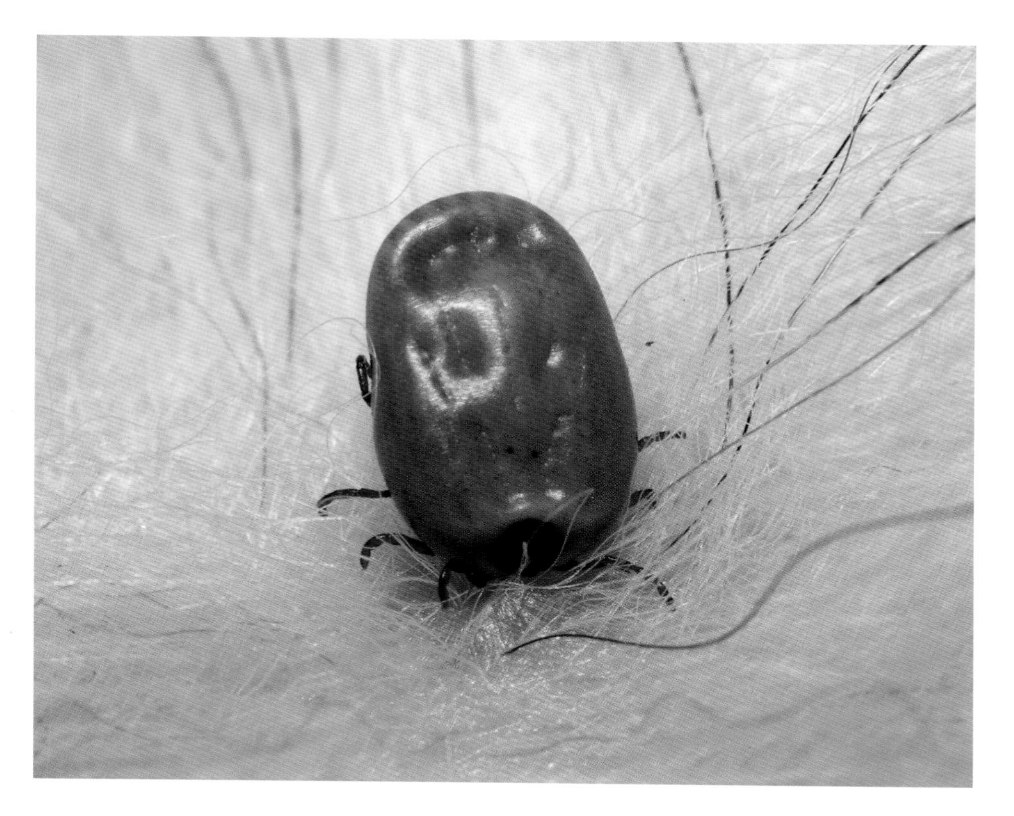

LEFT: *A brown tick attached to the skin of a dog, feeding on its blood*

EIGHT-LEGGED BLOODSUCKERS

Fleas are not the only buggy bloodsuckers at the parasite party. Ticks, too, are like little vampires. These eight-legged critters survive by slurping the blood of deer, horses, small reptiles, and, yes, humans.

When not gobbling gobs of blood from its hosts, ticks live in tall grass and shrubs. When an unsuspecting animal or person brushes by, ticks hop on the animal's fur, skin, or clothes. Like fleas, ticks can sense a host's body heat and can detect the carbon dioxide it exhales.

Unlike fleas, though, ticks cannot jump high to catch their hosts. All they can do is crawl. So, once onboard, they crawl and crawl until they find a warm, out of the way spot to jab in its *hypostome*, and start drinking. The hypostome is like a tiny harpoon. It has sharp, angled bristles that help secure the tick into the skin. After sticking in its hypostome, the tick also releases a sticky goo that helps lock itself in place.

Fun Fact!

Given that both fleas and ticks are tiny pests that feed on blood, you would think that they're closely related. But ticks aren't even insects. They're actually a cousin of the spider and belong to a group called *arachnids* that have four pairs of legs. (Insects have only three pairs.)

Usually, after a few days, when the tick is full of blood, it drops off the host's body. The adult female tick needs a large three-day "blood buffet" before she can reproduce and lay her 2,000 or more eggs.

What ticks take from their hosts (blood) is not as bad as what they sometimes leave (diseases). Bacteria that live inside some kinds of ticks can be passed to their host's blood when the tick attaches its body. One of the most well-known of these diseases is Lyme disease, which is often carried by the deer tick. Deer ticks are about the same size as the head of a pin.

During the early stages of Lyme disease, an infected person might feel sore muscles or joints, feel very tired, or have chills or fever. Some people with Lyme disease have a skin rash that looks like a small red circle. But other infected people don't have these early symptoms. If you think you've been bitten by a tick, tell an adult immediately. An adult or doctor can help you remove the tick (if it is still there). If you save the tick in a jar, you can show it to your doctor. Usually, if a tick is removed within twenty-four hours, then it doesn't have time to spread any diseases it is carrying.

Which is cleaner—a dog's mouth or yours?

As you know from the first chapter, your mouth is home to millions of bacteria. Most of these bacteria are harmless, and the ones that aren't are usually taken care of by regular brushing and flossing. As you may have noticed, dogs aren't as careful about their oral hygiene. According to some people, dogs' mouths are, in general, cleaner than humans. These people obviously haven't given a lot of thought to where dogs usually put their tongues, or what kinds of things dogs will happily stick in their mouths. Veterinarian Gary Clemons points out, "A dog's mouth contains a lot of bacteria. Remember, a dog's tongue is not only his washcloth but also his toilet paper." Yuck!

Protecting Yourself from Lyme Disease

When you or your pets spend time in a forest or woodsy area, particularly where many deer live, make sure to protect yourself against a tickborne illness. Here are some tips for avoiding tick bites, and the proper way to remove them from your clothes and body if they attach themselves to you.

Before you go

Wear long-sleeve shirts, long pants, and sturdy shoes. Tuck your pants into your socks. You might even use tape to close the area between pants and socks. Wear light-colored clothing, so you can spot ticks more quickly.

While in the woods

Look for ticks every two to three hours. If you spot any ticks' crawling on your clothes, use masking or cellophane tape to remove them. Don't use your bare fingers (d'uh!). Ticks take time to attach themselves (and to pass along any diseases the might be carrying). So, if you remove a tick within a few hours of its arrival, you have a smaller chance of getting any infectious diseases from it.

Removing ticks

Remember, the ticks' mouthparts are barbed. If you just yank out the tick, there's a good chance that part of its body (and its nasty microbes) will stay inside you. The best way to remove a tick is to first clean the area with hydrogen peroxide. Then, hold its body with tweezers as close to the skin as possible. Pull it gently but firmly out without twisting its body. (Most pet stores carry special tools to help remove ticks.) To kill the removed tick, put it in rubbing alcohol or flush it down the toilet. Once the tick is removed, put more hydrogen peroxide where the tick attached itself. Wash your hands and disinfect the tweezers by putting it in alcohol. Here are many bad ways to remove a tick that some people claim will work. They don't, and can cause infection. Don't put Vaseline on them, gasoline on them, or burn them off with a match.

Be on the lookout

If you or your pet develop any symptoms such as fever, rash, headaches, or muscle aches three to thirty days after the tick was removed, see your doctor. Some people get a rash that looks like a bull's-eye, but others have no rash at all. A simple blood test can usually tell you if you were infected.

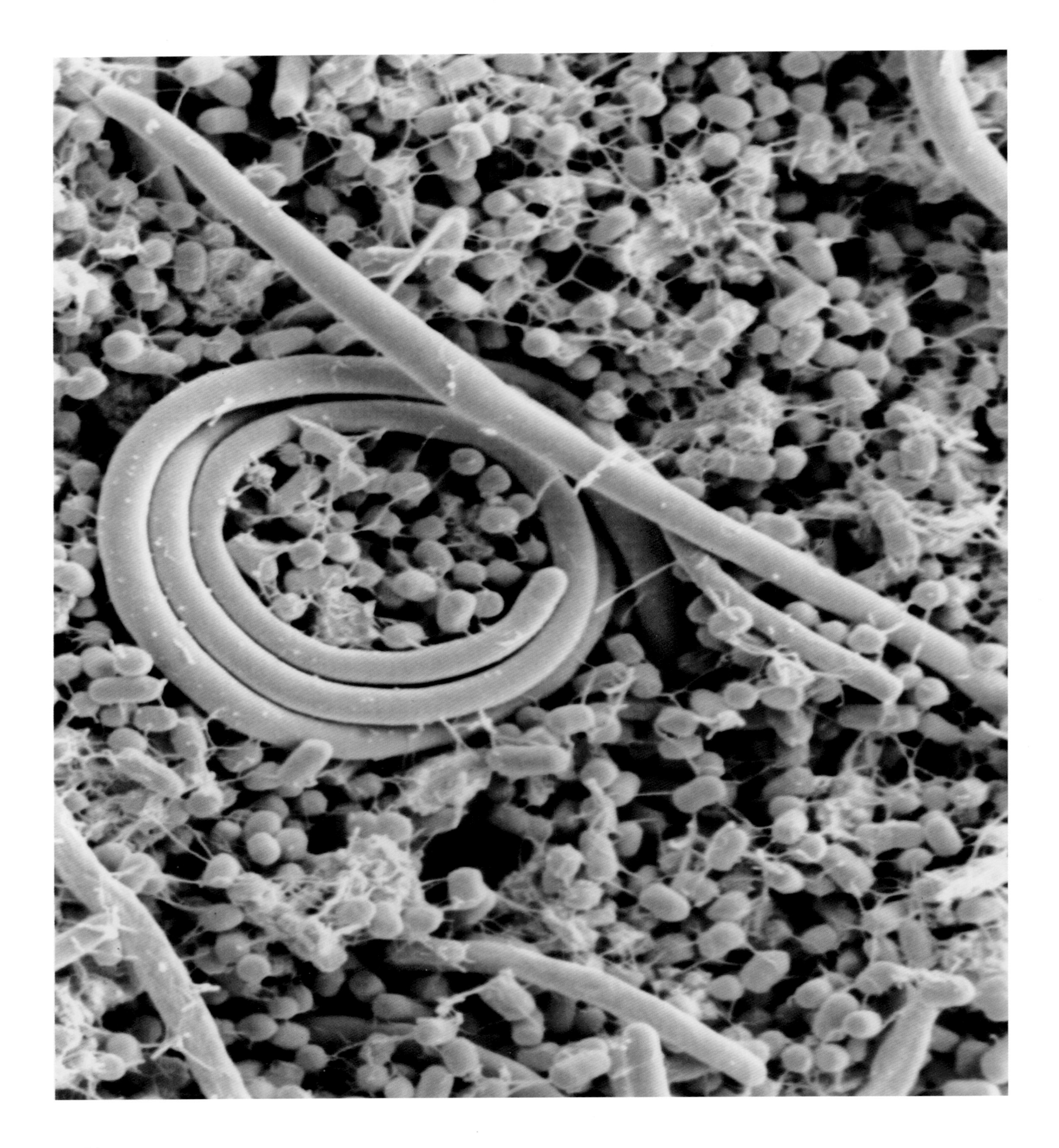

THE TROUBLE WITH TURTLES

Turtles can make wonderful pets. They have colorful shells, are easy to take care of, and can live many years. But many people don't realize that when you bring a turtle into your home, there's a good chance you're also inviting millions of tiny *Salmonella* bacteria. While these bacteria usually don't harm the turtles they live on, they can make people sick. If someone gets *Salmonella* in their bodies, they might vomit, get bloody diarrhea, have a fever or bad headache, and even need to see a doctor to get antibiotics to treat it.

The best way to protect yourself from *Salmonella* is to wash your hands with warm soap and water after you play with a turtle.

OPPOSITE PAGE: Salmonella *bacteria don't only live on turtles. This kind of bacteria can also be found in some raw eggs. That is why medical experts discourage people from eating raw cookie dough. Since the chances of getting* Salmonella *from a fresh egg are quite slim, some cookie-dough lovers take the risk.*

CHAPTER 4

Creatures of the Kitchen

You wake up in the middle of the night. The moonlight shines through your bedroom window, casting creepy shadows against the wall. Sweat drips from every part of your body. The shadows appear to be taunting you. "That's not really a monster!" you say to yourself. "It's just my imagination." But if there are no spooky creatures, then what is that eerie growling noise? You hide your head under the covers, but the low-pitched rumbling continues. You're about to wake up your family, when suddenly it hits you—that sound is just your stomach. You're hungry. Time for a little snack.

You tiptoe into the kitchen, wondering if you already ate the last chocolate chip cookie. You flip on the light switch, and tons of little bugs scurry into their hiding places. In seconds, the kitchen appears totally critter free. But don't think for a minute that you're the only living thing interested in a midnight snack.

Like it or not, most kitchens are crawling with life. In addition to maybe some furry little mice, there could be millions of smaller creatures lurking in your kitchen 24/7, feasting on a smorgasbord of your leftovers. Some are tiny insects or spiders you can barely see, but most of your "snack mates" are microscopic. The good news is most of these bugs and microbes are harmless. The bad news is that some of these kitchen creatures can make you very sick. So kick back and grab a snack, as this chapter presents you the good, the bad, and the yucky.

BUGS YOU CAN SEE WITHOUT A MICROSCOPE

Imagine you're a tiny insect or spider. If you were playing hide-and-seek in your kitchen with another bug your size, where would be some good hiding places? Perhaps you'd squeeze into a cozy crack in a wall? Wiggling your way under the refrigerator might work—people never go there. Ooh, what about under the oven? So many choices!

Before we get into the microscopic creatures, let's meet the visible bugs. These little guys look at the grunge in a garbage can, the piled up grease on the stove, and the specks of food in the microwave . . . and think, "Yum! There's no place like home."

Ants

Ants have been invading picnics for as long as people have been having them. These six-legged insects are crazy about sugar but love other kinds of human food, too. In places where the weather gets chilly, ants make our homes their homes. If you're an ant, you're going to pick the room with the most food—the kitchen.

When ants find some tasty grub, such as an open box of sugary cereal, they send the word to the hundreds of other ants nearby. Ants communicate with each other by touching their antennae. They also leave "scent clues" for each other by spraying special chemicals where they've walked. Other ants smell these chemicals, and know where to go to find a tasty meal. Ants live in large groups called a *colony*, led by a queen

While ants are very strong creatures, they can't actually lift large pieces of fruit.

ant, which rarely leaves the nest. To get the food back to the colony sometimes requires lots of lifting and carrying.

Luckily, ants are very strong for their size, and can run fast when necessary. If you've ever squashed an ant, you may have wondered why you didn't see any blood squirt out. They actually do have blood but it isn't red like ours; it's clear.

Wow! Some Amazing Roach Facts!

- The Death Head Cockroach has six brains. Only one is in its head; the rest are in its legs.
- If a cockroach loses its head, it can survive for a week. Eventually, it dies of thirst.
- The oldest cockroach fossil is 350 million years old. That's 150 million years before the first known dinosaurs walked on our planet.

Cockroaches

Cockroaches are among the most famous kitchen critters. All they need to survive is food, water, and a place to hide. For food, they can eat almost anything, including bits of rotten meat, rat droppings, soap, and cardboard. Their small, flat bodies are excellent at hiding in small cracks. A young cockroach can squeeze into a crack that's as thin as a dime. While cockroaches prefer messy kitchens, they can do just fine in neater ones. Some roaches survive by hiding under the labels of canned foods, and eating the glue on the labels.

Not being picky about its meals has helped cockroaches survive on Earth for millions of years. There were even cockroaches around before the first dinosaurs appeared, and many kinds of cockroaches survived when other creatures became extinct.

Since roaches often hang out in garbage cans and sewers, their bodies can pick up harmful bacteria along the way. The problem for humans comes when these germ-covered roaches then take a stroll across our plates, forks, and spatulas.

The German cockroach is the one that gives all cockroaches a bad reputation. These roaches are commonly found in U.S. kitchens, especially in apartment buildings in big cities.

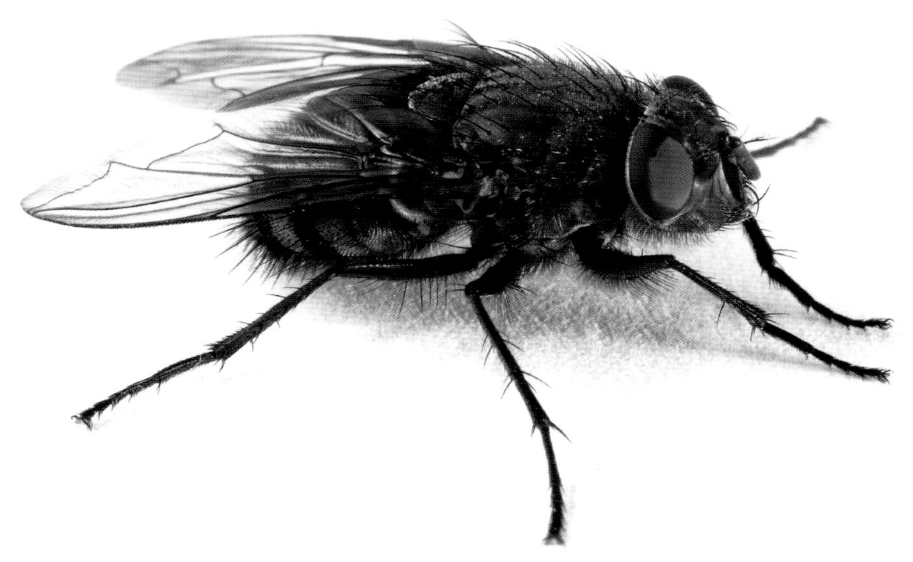

LEFT: *Close-up of a housefly*
BOTTOM: *Silverfish* (Lepisma saccharina)

Houseflies

When a fly lands on your hotdog, guess what it's probably doing? Throwing up! Adult houseflies have straw-like mouths, and can only drink their meals. So, if a fly wants to chow down on something solid, it first has to vomit chemicals on the food to break it down into a liquid. Oh, and when flies are not busy barfing on your food, they are probably going to the bathroom on it.

It gets worse. Flies usually hang out and lay their eggs in a variety of gross places including animal poop, rotting fruits and vegetables, and garbage cans. While there, their six little feet often pick up harmful bacteria, such as dysentery, cholera, and tuberculosis, that can make you very sick.

Whoa! Fly Facts!

Female houseflies live about two-and-a-half months. During this time, each mother fly can lay over 9,000 eggs. These eggs usually become grownup flies in less than two weeks.

Silverfish

It's easy to see why librarians hate silverfish. These little wingless insects are famous for dining on the glue that binds books together. At night, these bugs also enjoy nibbling on old photographs, wallpaper paste, fabric, sugar, cereal hair, and dandruff. The silverfish gets its name from its silvery blue color, long body, and its fish-like movements. It prefers damp, cool places, like basements. Amazingly, the silverfish can survive for a year without food.

Flour beetles sometimes eat dry pet food.

Flour Beetles

The next time you're baking cookies, be careful not to add a secret crunchy ingredient to your batter: bugs! Flour beetles, about 3/16 inch (.5 cm) long, are common in kitchens and flour-producing plants. If given the chance, they'll hang out in your breakfast cereal or containers of various grains. And these are hearty buggers. The science TV show *MythBusters* did an awesome experiment in which flour bugs were exposed to super deadly radiation—100 times more powerful than what would kill humans. Guess what happened. About 10% of the flour beetles in this experiment survived! And you can bet that if given the chance, they'll make more "super" flour beetles.

Sawtoothed Grain Beetle

These little guys, about 1/8 inch (3.2 mm) long, can be found nibbling on dried fruit, nuts, macaroni, and seeds. Their sharp little mouths have no trouble breaking into sealed packages. On the bright side, they do not bite or sting humans, they don't usually spread disease, and they usually don't damage furniture.

Indianmeal Moths

Indianmeal moths are sneaky hitchhikers. Unlike ants, which enter a home by crawling in from outside, these insects enter kitchens by traveling inside food products. If someone accidentally buys a container of nuts that is infested with these moths, then they can lay eggs and raise a big Indianmeal moth family in your home. This little critter, about an inch long when its wings are spread, might hitchhike in a bag of flour, a box of cake mix, or a bag of dog food. It gets its name because it used to break into containers of Indian corn, also known as maize. This moth is most active at night, but it loves the light, so they might hover near a bulb in the kitchen.

Spiders

Are you scared of spiders? Many people are. But many of us forget that most spiders are not only harmless, but help humans by gobbling our pests. Spiders such as the common house spider dine on a variety of pests like mosquitos or flies that would love to nibble your food.

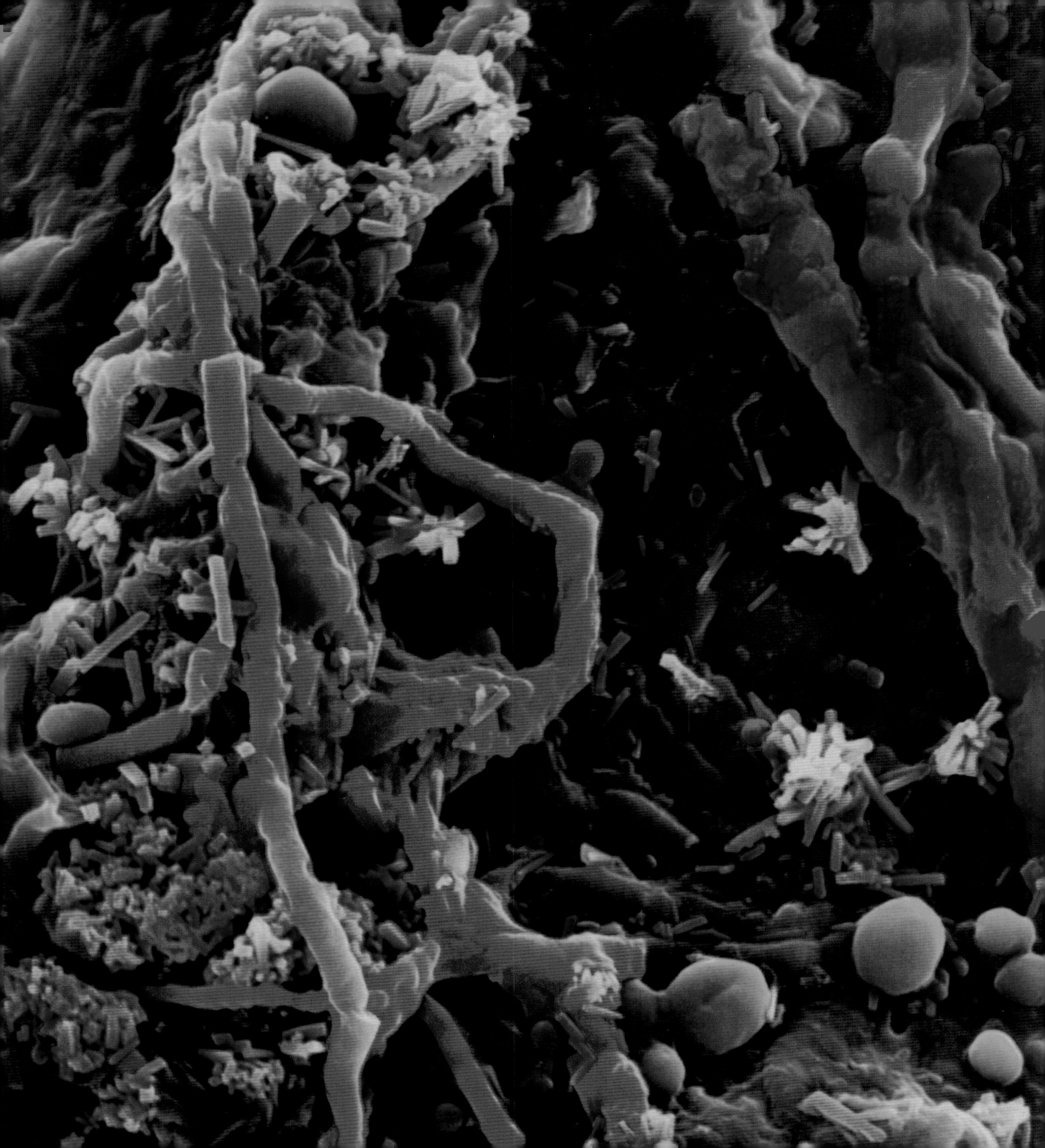

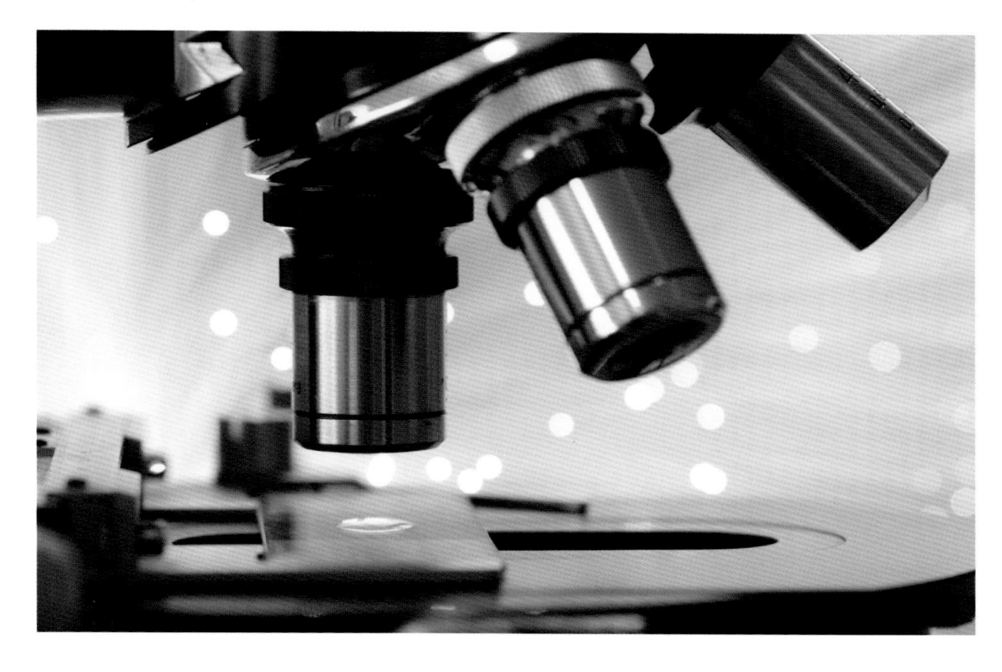

INVISIBLE INVADERS

If you could look at your kitchen through a super-powered microscope, you'd probably be shocked by the number of microbes living in places that you thought were clean. Take the kitchen sink, for example. Some scientists found that most kitchen sinks have more bacteria than bathroom sinks. They also found that most kitchen towels and sponges were loaded with harmful bacteria. Surprised? Most of us think of sponges and cloth towels as tools to help us clean up. But when we use a bacteria-filled sponge to wash a cup or spoon, we are actually spreading the germs to something we might put in our mouths. Yuck! Microbiologist Charles Gerba explains that "Bacteria find a happy home in sponges. When you wipe, you take up food and drink and bacteria can feed on that." In a study, Gerba found that a flushed toilet bowl was actually cleaner than most kitchen sinks. Think about it: Many people make a point of cleaning their toilet bowls with bleach and other strong chemicals. But these folks don't realize that when they clean raw chicken in the sink, or wash off leftovers down the drain, they are actually allowing bacteria to live and grow there.

OPPOSITE PAGE: *A wet, dirty sponge provides the perfect environment for a host of microbes to grow, such as the bacteria and fungi show here. The microbes' waste products are what make a sponge so stinky. This image was magnified nearly 600x.*

TRY THIS! *Zap a Germy Sponge*

If you were a bacterium, you and your family would probably find a used sponge a wonderful place to live. It's got everything you'd want—tiny bits of food and water, and tons of little crevices to grow. That's why if you were the human owner of this used sponge, you'd be wise to *sterlize* it daily. When you sterilize a sponge with heat or chemicals, you kill off all the harmful bacteria. Some microbe-murdering researchers at the University of Florida discovered this fascinating fact: If you stick a wet sponge in a microwave oven, and zap it on high for two minutes, you'll kill practically all the bacteria, viruses, and spores on the sponge! (These intrepid researchers even tried this out with a sponge that had been sitting in raw sewage! And it worked.)

To sterilize a sponge at home, here's all you have to do.

1. IMPORTANT: For safety, have a grownup nearby—just in case.
2. Make sure the used sponge is good and wet, and doesn't contain any metal. (Otherwise, you could cause a fire or damage the microwave.)
3. Zap the sponge for no more than two minutes—and keep an eye on it as it is being cooked.
4. After the microwave stops, wash your hands. (No point in touching a freshly sterilized sponge with germy hands, right?)
5. Wait for at least ten minutes, then remove the sponge from the microwave. Be very careful, especially when squeezing out any leftover water—the water could be hot.

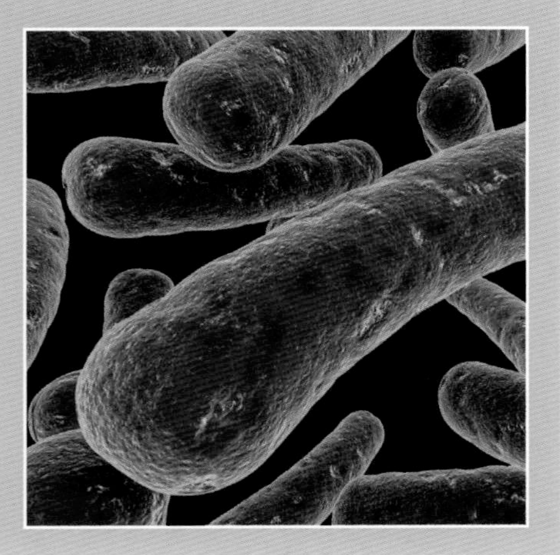

Gerba was also surprised to discover that single guys who lived like slobs actually had cleaner kitchens than those conscientious "neat freaks" who spent hours carefully scrubbing their kitchens with a germy sponge. (Of course they didn't realize their sponges were dirty.)

Salute to . . . the sponge

Sponges are all about cleaning, right? Not all the time. Sponges can be effective cleaning tools when they are new or have been washed in very hot water. But in many homes, sponges do an amazing job at spreading germs. Just rinsing out a dirty sponge in cold water won't kill the micro-critters lurking inside.

One of the most common germs found in kitchen sponges is *E. coli*. This kind of bacteria might look like a scary alien from another world, but it is real—and eating your insides out! Okay, that's an exaggeration. Actually, *E. coli* is one of the kinds of bacteria that normally live in your gut. Inside the large

TRY THIS! *Making Mold*

Have you ever seen bluish-green blobs on your bread? If so, don't eat it. That's mold. Mold is a type of fungus, like a mushroom, but is much, much smaller. The reason you can see the mold is that there are millions and millions of molds, connected together in a colony. Sometimes mold grows by accident—here's a way to grow it on purpose.

What to Do

1. Put a piece of fresh bread in a sealable plastic bag. (You can also put it in a plastic container, and cover it with plastic wrap.)
2. Sprinkle a few drops of water on the bread, or put a wet paper towel next to the bread.
3. Leave the bread exposed to the air for an hour.
4. Then zip the bag closed (or put the plastic wrap on top). Leave a tiny hole for air to circulate.
5. Put the bread bag or container in a dark place at room temperature.
6. Check on the bag every day. In a few days, you should start to see some mold growing. Important: Once the mold starts to grow, don't open the container.

Electron micrograph of a cluster of E. coli *bacteria. Each rod-shaped object is a single bacterium.*

intestine (colon) of warm-blooded animals, such as cows, dogs, or humans, *E. coli* and other microbes help us digest food and produce essential vitamins. When poop comes out of your body, it contains countless *E. coli*. (Told you it was a good idea to wash your hands before you eat!)

Most of the time, *E. coli* and humans live happily together. But when some rare types of *E. coli* get into our blood, it can lead to trouble—bad stomach cramps, vomiting, bloody diarrhea, or worse. You might be wondering: How can these harmful bacteria get inside your blood? One way might be if you eat an undercooked hamburger that was made from the beef of an infected cow. Or you might have forgotten to wash your hands after touching some ground beef that is home to some harmful *E. coli*. Still another way might be if you swallowed a carrot or apple that wasn't cleaned properly or was sliced on the same cutting board that was used for preparing raw meat.

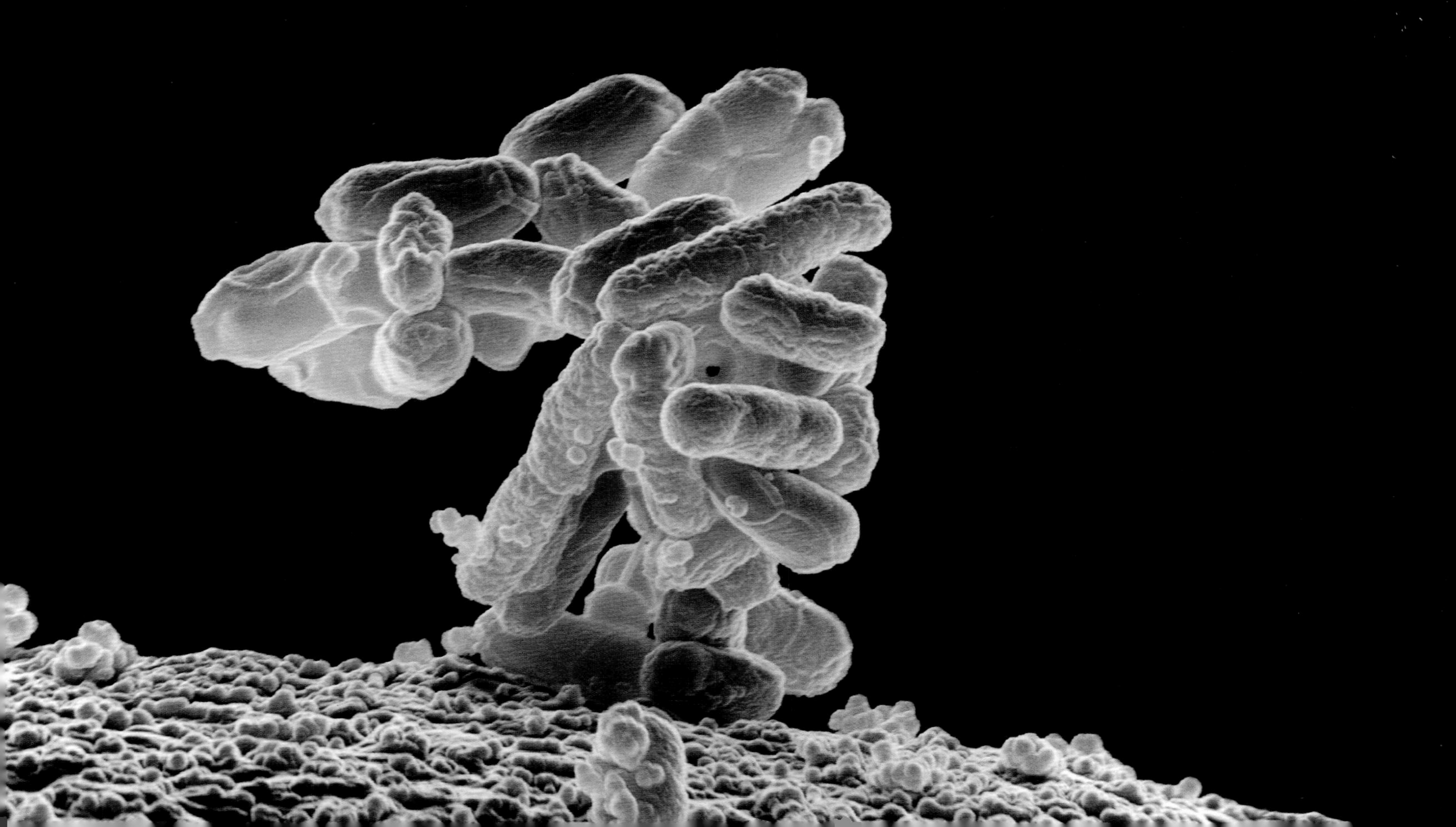

CHAPTER

Places Germs Hide . . . and How You Can Seek Them!

Imagine a wealthy scientist knocked on your door and said, "I'll give you a million dollars if you can find the top five places in your home that have the most germs. What would you do? Since the little creatures the scientist challenged you to find are invisible without a microscope, how could you track down their hotspots? In the last chapter, you found out that the kitchen is a favorite microbe hangout. But what other rooms are clogged with those disgusting little bacteria?

To find the answer, think about the kind of environment these microbes like. In general, if a room is cold, dry, and clean, there probably won't be a bunch of bacteria lurking there. But if a room is warm, wet, and dirty—BINGO!—that room is probably Bacteria City. If that room also has little bits of dead skin on the floors, even better! Throw in some tiny food scraps, some bits of poop, some garbage, and there's an excellent chance that billions of bacteria are swarming in that room—and making billions of baby bacteria.

BACTERIA IN THE BATHROOM

Next stop on the microscopic tour of your home . . . the bathroom. Most people might guess that the toilet is most germ-infested part of the average bathroom. It makes perfect sense. The toilet's the place, after all, where people poop, pee, barf, and toss out gross things like used tissues.

It turns out, though, that a flushed toilet is actually one of the cleanest places in most bathrooms. Bathroom sinks, on the other hand, are much more germ-covered. Surprised? Think about it. Most people make a point of cleaning their toilets fairly often, and even put strong chemicals in there like bleach. Bathroom sinks, on the other hand, *look* pretty clean, so they rarely get the ol' scrub-a-dub. But when you brush and floss

This bathroom may look sparkly clean, but is it really microbe-free?

your teeth, you spit out bits of food, often mixed with a small amount of blood from your gums. Only some of this food and blood go down the drain. The rest hang around the sink and inside the drain, where it attracts bacteria that feed on these disgusting leftovers. Bacteria also love old, crusty toothpaste that sticks to sinks.

Bathroom floors can also be really germy because they are usually cleaned even less often than toilets and sinks. Think about how floors collect the kinds of food that bacteria eat. When people come home, they often leave their shoes on, so they track in tons of dirt, germs, and grime from outside. All this yucky stuff gets stuck in carpets and on floors throughout the house. Even when we walk around barefoot, we can track dirt and germs from room to room, and shed old skin from your feet. When you flush a toilet without the lid down, tiny bits of dirty water spray up into the air, and land on—the floor. After a bath or shower, when you dry off your body, you're probably scraping old bits of skin on the floor.

The Five-Second Rule

While on the topic of floors, let's talk about the so-called Five-Second Rule. Some kids and grownups actually believe that if you drop a piece of food on the floor, it is safe to eat if you pick it up within five seconds. That's nonsense! If bacteria could laugh, they would. Anything that touches the floor needs to be washed well before you put it in your mouth. Otherwise, you could swallow germs that could make you sick.

If you think the bathroom floor at home is disgusting, bathrooms in public places are even worse! Just ask Dr. Charles Gerba. He's a scientist who studies little life forms like bacteria. For his job, he visited public bathrooms with some special germ-detecting tools. Here are some of his discoveries:

- Two places that germ freaks worry about most in public bathrooms—the toilet seat and the doorknob—were actually the cleanest places. (These normally germy places were cleaned the most by custodians.)

- Women's bathrooms usually had much more bacteria than men's bathrooms. Why? First, men's bathrooms usually have urinals, but women's bathrooms have only toilets. And, as a rule, more bacteria grow on toilets than urinals. Another reason is that women's rooms are used more often to change diapers. And old poopy diapers are definitely loaded with bacteria.

- The stalls farthest away from the main door of the bathroom had more germs in them than the first stall. Dr. Gerba suspected that this is because more people use the back stalls for privacy.

- It's a *bad* idea to put your backpack or purse on a bathroom

When a toilet is flushed with the seat up, microbes can escape in the tiny water spray. That's why it's wise to keep your toothbrush in the cabinet.

floor. Gerba found 30% of woman's purses had fecal bacteria (poop) on the bottom of them. That's because the bacteria that eat poop usually live on the floor of public bathrooms. Here's a gross thought: What if a mother puts her purse on the floor of a public bathroom while she's using it, then comes home and puts this bag on the kitchen counter? Then she makes a sandwich on that counter, and . . . yeeech. We'll leave the rest to your imagination.

- While hot-air dryers save more trees than paper towel dispensers, they are not necessarily more sanitary. Gerba found that hot-air dryers actually help blast germy bacteria around the bathroom, so they land on your freshly cleaned hands.

Which Is Cleaner?

Which do you think is covered with more germs? The equipment at a public playground . . . or the toilet seat of a non-flushable port-o-potty? One study found that the port-o-potty seat in one study was *much* cleaner than the playground equipment. Why? The port-o-potty companies clean their products much more often than playground equipment is cleaned. When is the last time you saw someone scrub down a slide or swing? Think of all the little kids who touch the playground equipment with their germy hands, especially during cold season. Don't panic about going to the neighborhood playground, but make sure you wash your hands afterward, especially before having a snack!

TRY THIS! *Go on a Microbe Scavenger Hunt*

Do you want to know what kinds of bacteria are lurking in your mouth, on the toilet seat, or on the doorknob to your bedroom? This experiment will give you some answers. Each bacterium is way too small to see without a microscope, but if you grow enough of them, together they become visible! To grow bacteria safely, you'll need to buy round, flat plastic containers called *petri* [PEET-ree] dishes. Like any living thing, bacteria need food to survive. For this experiment, you'll be feeding your "homemade" creatures something called *agar* [AW-gur], a powder made from seaweed. Petri dishes and agar are easily available online. You might also check with a science teacher.

What you need

- 4 inch (10.2 cm) size petri dishes
- agar powder
- water
- quart-size plastic or glass bowl, safe for boiling water in a microwave oven
- microwave oven
- plastic wrap
- permanent marker
- clean cotton swabs
- bleach, or bleach spray
- adult to help out

What to do

1. In a microwave-safe mixing bowl, mix together ½ teaspoon of agar with ⅓ cup of hot water from the sink. With the help of an adult, boil this mixture for 1 minute in a microwave oven, until the agar is completely dissolved. Don't let the solution boil over.
2. Cool the mixture for 5 minutes on a counter. With the help of an adult, pour half the agar solution into one half of the petri dish; then repeat with the other half. Cover each petri dish half with plastic wrap. Let it cool for an hour, until the solution has hardened.
3. Time to collect some bacteria! Rub a clean cotton swab over any gross place you can think of—between your unbrushed teeth, the toilet seat, doorknob, computer keyboard, etc. Use a permanent marker to label the bottom of each petri dish half. You might write, for example, "mouth" or "toilet seat cover." Since you can't see the bacteria yet, you'll have to trust that you "caught" some on your swab. Remember to use a clean cotton swab for each collection.
4. For each sample, remove the plastic wrap from each half of the petri dish and gently draw a squiggly line in the agar with the end of the swab. Cover each half with the plastic wrap again. Place the dishes in a warm, dark place that is no hotter than 98°F (37°C).
5. Now the hard part—wait. In a few days, microbes will start to grow enough that you'll be able to see a variety of bacteria, molds, fungi, and more. To be safe, keep the plastic wrap on your dishes, and never breathe in near growing bacteria.
6. When your experiment is done, you can kill off your bacteria colonies by having an adult pour bleach on them.

Hard to imagine what this shower looked like before it was invaded by mold, mildew, and more.

BACTERIA'S BATHROOM BUDDIES

Have you ever noticed mysterious black gunk on your shower curtain? If you watch the curtain carefully over the course of a few weeks (and don't clean it), you'll see the gunk creep across more and more of your curtain. You can also spot this weird black stuff in dark linen closets and wet laundry baskets. What *is* it? Oh, just bacteria's bathroom buddy—*mildew.* Mildew is a type of fungus that grows in warm, moist environments, and thrives when the temperature is between 75° and 85°F (24° and 29°C). It's often black and grows the most in places where the air circulates the least.

Micro-Life on Your Toothbrush

If you're healthy, a toothbrush can do a great job cleaning your teeth for about three months. After that time, dentists recommend you replace it. Otherwise, bacteria and other little creatures can grow, and you'll be spreading them in your mouth each time you brush. If you swallow too many of these germs, you can get a bad cold, or worse.

By the way, did you know that before the invention of the toothbrush and minty toothpaste, people had wacky ways of cleaning their teeth? Long ago, some people brushed with ground-up chalk, lemon juice, ashes, and a mixture of tobacco and honey. Eeew!

Bugs in the Bedroom

Every hour, your skin does something pretty amazing—and pretty disgusting. It lets go of more than a million dead skin cells. These old skin cells fall in your clothes, on the floor, on the furniture, everywhere. Your skin is also a powerful sweat factory, releasing about a quart of sweat each day.

While the thought of all that dead skin flaking off your body might make you feel like throwing up, there are some little creatures that are thrilled. These microscopic bugs are called *dust mites*. They live in your mattress and pillow and *love*

Dinnertime for this dust mite. The dust it eats is made of dead skin cells, dried bug feces, and the dead bodies of other little creatures. Yum!

If your vision were 100x stronger, you could see dust mites like these.

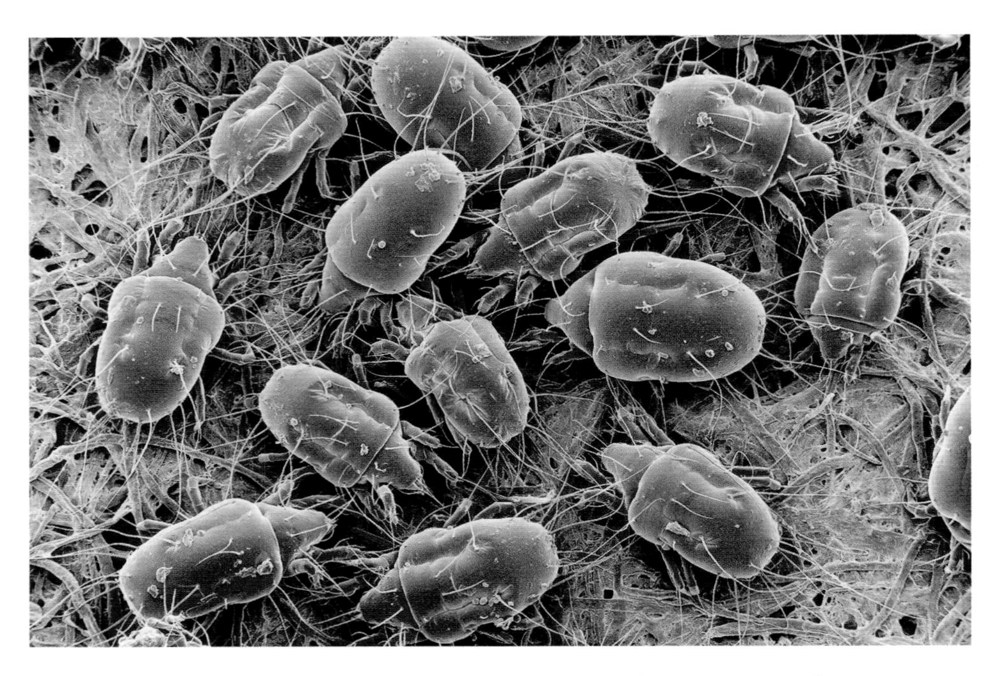

nibbling old dead skin. If you have a pet dog or cat at home, even more for dust mites to chow down on. The average mattress contains tens of thousands of dust mites. Just one dust mite poops about twenty times a day. Don't worry, though. Dust mites are usually harmless, except for some individuals who are allergic to their droppings, or have bad asthma. Dust mites are actually doing a helpful job for us. They get rid of all that dead skin we shed. Some people are allergic to dust mite poop, and become itchy, or find it hard to breathe if too many of these micro-bugs are around. To help the situation, there are special airtight pillow and mattress covers that keep dust mites off our bodies. Other ways to reduce the number of dust mites is to keep down the clutter in a bedroom, keep stuffed toys off beds, and keep the room as dry as possible.

You may have heard your parents say, "Don't let the bedbugs bite!" just before you get ready for a good night's rest. If you always thought this was just a silly expression, here's some bad news: Bedbugs are real, and they can live in bedrooms by the hundreds, or more. Unlike dust mites, which live in most bedrooms, bedbugs only affect some homes. But once they settle into a home or an apartment building, they can be very tricky to get rid of.

Bedbugs are flat, reddish-brown, wingless insects a bit smaller than a raisin. During the day, they hide in the walls, in tiny cracks, behind electrical outlets, underneath wallpaper, behind picture frames, and more. But at night, they slip out through the cracks and come to feast on blood . . . your blood.

Bedbugs can find us in the dark by sensing the carbon dioxide gas we breathe out. Once they find a sleeping human, they stick their mouthparts into our skin, and suck away. Bedbugs are hearty eaters. In less than fifteen minutes of blood-sucking, their bodies can triple in size.

Even if we're not asleep, we may not feel a thing because the bedbug's saliva contains a special painkiller. Bedbug spit also contains a special ingredient that keeps our blood flowing freely. (Normally, when you get a cut, your body's blood naturally clots to slow the flow.) In the morning, the bite left by a bedbug might look like a small red dot and feel itchy. If you think you've been bitten by bedbugs, don't panic and try not to

An adult bedbug sucking blood from a human host

No Food? I Can Wait!

Bedbugs can survive for many months without eating!

scratch. Just wash the area with soap and water, and ask an adult to help get you some anti-itch cream.

If a home has a big bedbug problem, it may be necessary to hire an exterminator to spray special chemicals to kill off these sneaky critters. And remember, just getting rid of the bugs isn't enough. It's important to get rid of all their eggs, too. Bedbugs hide their tiny eggs in blankets, soft furniture, and even inside favorite stuffed animals.

GERMS GO FOR A SWIM

Have you ever wondered why people put chlorine in swimming pools? Chorine is a very strong chemical that keeps some tiny creatures from growing there. Pool filters and pumps also help keep a pool's water clean and microbe-free.

If you left a big pool of water alone for a while, and didn't add any chemicals, here are some of the little life forms that might grow there.

Algae

This is the stuff that can make the bottom of a clear pool look all greenish and yucky. Algae grow so fast that in less than a day, they can cover the bottom of a pool.

Green algae floating in a river

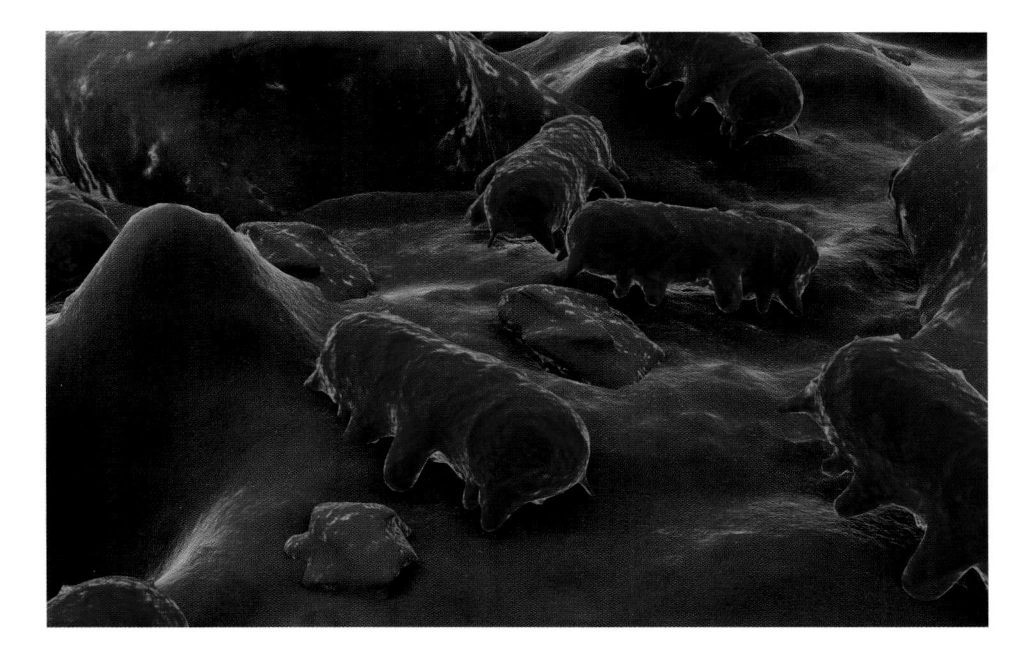

Color-treated photo of Salmonella *bacteria. About 40,000 cases of* Salmonella *infection are reported in the U.S. each year.*

Bacteria

Have you ever been in a public swimming pool and been asked to get out because someone accidentally pooped in it? Here's why: Normal poop contains bacteria that are harmful if swallowed or exposed to our eyes and nose. If a swimmer releases diarrhea in a public pool, other swimmers might get the diarrhea-causing microbes, including *Giardia* and *Salmonella*.

Remember that wealthy scientist from the beginning of this chapter? Would you now be able to win that million dollars by finding the germiest places in your home?

If your home is like most homes in America, then the top five germiest places are probably:

- The kitchen sink
- Used sponges (not sterilized)
- Bathtub
- Wet laundry (from washing machine—but without bleach)
- Toilet (maybe toilet handles since most people flush *before* washing up)

Famous Germaphobes

While it is smart to wash your hands after you go to the bathroom and before you eat, you can definitely go too far.

Here are some famous germophobes—and what they do:

- Actress Cameron Diaz opens doors with her elbows.
- Business superstar Donald Trump avoids shaking hands in public.
- Howie Mandel built a guesthouse where he stays when his kids are sick.
- Actress Katie Holmes sprays playground equipment with disinfectant before she lets her daughter play on it.
- NFL player Randy Moss avoids touching doorknobs and won't let anyone open his refrigerator without washing their hands.
- TV personality Nicole Ritchie always washes all her daughter's clothes, baby bottles, and spoons twice before using them.
- Actress Gwyneth Paltrow scrubs the bathrooms at hotels where she's staying.

CHAPTER

Swimming with Plankton

Imagine that you're scuba diving in the ocean. Swimming through the sea, you are dazzled by all the colorful creatures—sharks, dolphins, jellyfish, sea turtles, and much more. Then, in the distance, you spot an incredibly huge animal. As it swims near you, it looks longer than a school bus. Could it be? Yes, it's a humpback whale! At about 50 feet (15 m) long, it is one of the largest animals ever. While scientists have never put this mighty mammal on a scale, they estimate that it weighs as much as 40 tons.

THE BIGGEST EAT THE SMALLEST

Given its mammoth size, you might worry that this whale will gobble you up for lunch. Not a chance. It turns out that Earth's largest animal survives by eating some of the smallest creatures—a group of little shrimp-like animals known as *krill*. Most krill are only about 3/8 to 3/4 inch (1 to 2 cm) long. From the krill's point of view, you might look like a giant creature. In the ocean, these tiny, pink, almost see-through creatures gather in large groups called *swarms* or *clouds* that can make the ocean surface look pinkish. If all the plankton in the ocean disappeared suddenly, all the humpback whales would die out, too.

The Thrill of Krill

To get enough energy to survive, blue whales don't just nosh on krill—they *feast* on it. The average adult blue whale consumes about forty million krill a day (about 8,000 lbs/3,600 kg)! To get all these krill in their stomachs, blue whales rely on a special mouth filter called a *baleen*. To use it, a blue whale gulps tons of water, closes its mouth, then pushes the sea water back out through its baleen. This method keeps all the tasty krill inside

OPPOSITE PAGE: *This breaching humpback whale is enormous, but is small compared to the blue whale, which can be twice as big.*

Antarctic krill (Euphausia superba)
Most adult krill are tiny, about 1⁄3 to 3⁄4 inch (1 to 2 cm) long.

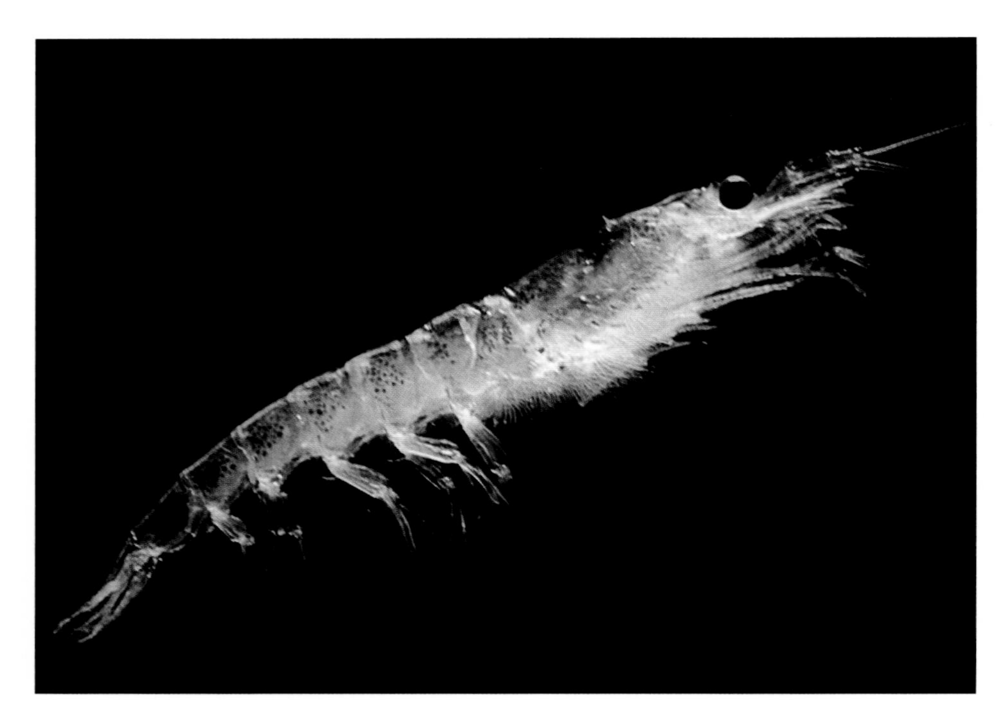

Thar She Blows . . . Peee-yeww!

Gulping down tons of tasty krill can lead to some rotten-smelling results. Like other mammals, when whales digest their food, their bodies need to release the extra gases as flatulence. Yup, we're talking about whale farts! On an expedition in Antarctica, a crew observed a minke whale letting one go. "We got away from the bow of the ship very quickly . . . it does stink," said Nick Gales, a research scientist onboard. What makes a whale's farts so stinky? Billions of bacteria in its gut!

the whale's mouth. After it swallows, the blue whale repeats the process again and again.

What Do Krill Eat?

When krill aren't busy being devoured by blue whales, these teeny-tiny creatures spend their time eating even littler living things called *plankton*. To say that all plankton are alike is as absurd as saying that all seventh graders are identical. Like middle school kids, plankton are a motley mix. First of all, plankton is a mix of tiny plants and mini-animals. The plant kind of plankton (known as *phytoplankton*) are single-celled organisms that float near the surface. Examples of phytoplankton include diatoms, golden algae, green algae, and cyanobacteria.

Krill are clever. Their instincts tell them that if they try to feed on surface plankton during the day, they'll get gobbled up by predators such as sea birds and whales. So when the sun is bright, they hang out hundreds of feet (about 320 feet or 100 meters) below the surface. In the dark of night, krill swim up to the surface to eat the phytoplankton. In their research, scientists have discovered that krill can go 200 days without eating. (While starving these little life forms sounds harsh, in the pursuit of scientific truth, you sometimes have to be "krill to be kind." Ahem.)

In addition to eating phytoplankton, some krill eat the animal kind of plankton, known as *zooplankton*. Some zooplankton are single-celled creatures such as foraminifera and protozoa, which range in size from about 10 micrometers to a "whopping" 1 millimeter. Other zooplankton are actually the "baby" versions of larger adult species, such as copepods, crabs, lobsters, jellyfish, sea cucumbers, and seastars. Zooplankton themselves gobble up phytoplankton, as well as other zooplankton.

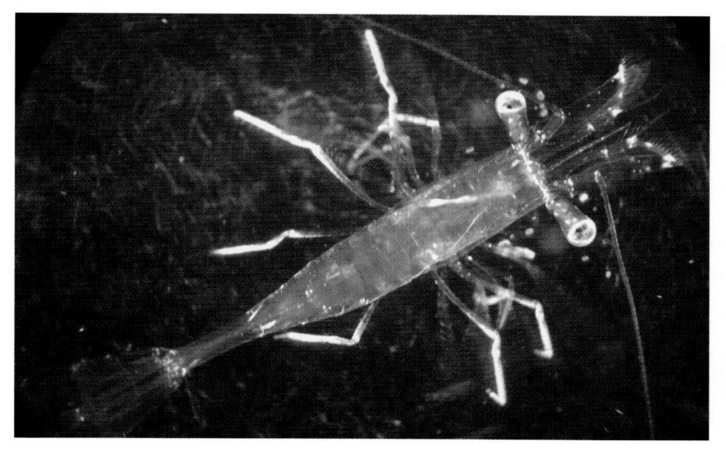

Lobster larva

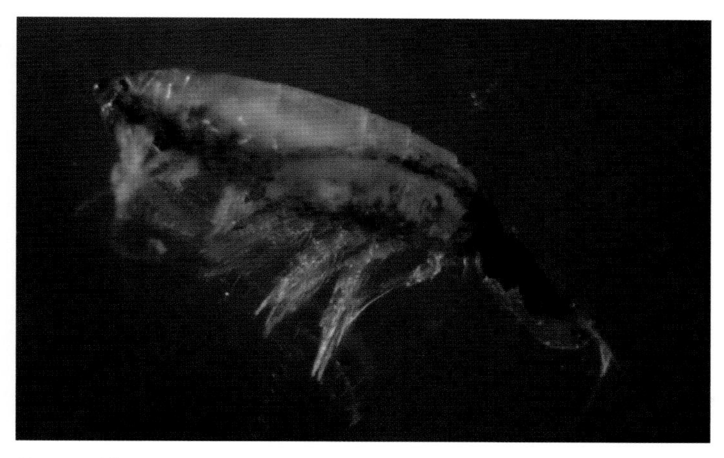

Copepod larva

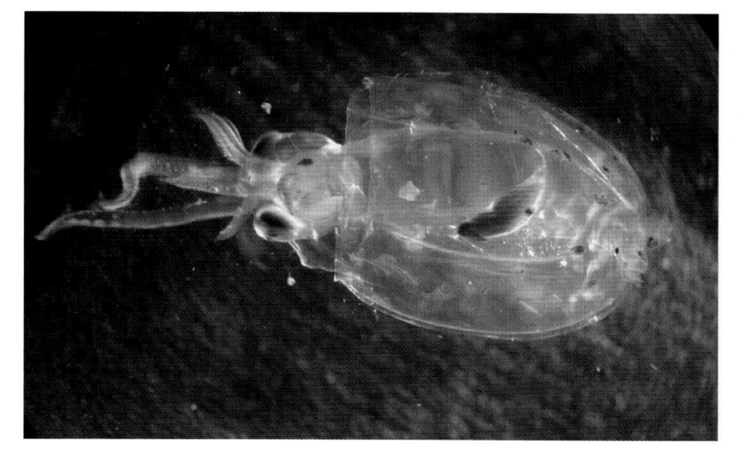

Octopus larva

Fish larvae

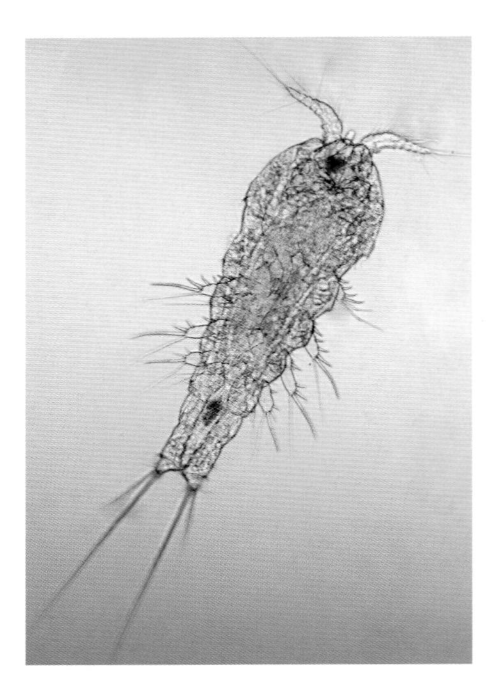

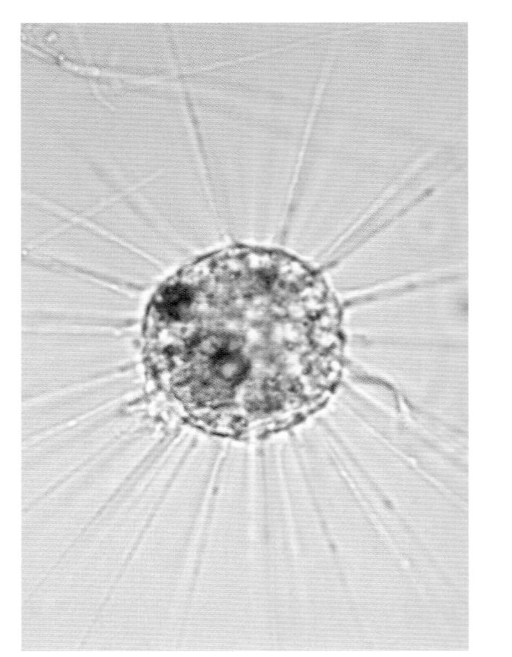

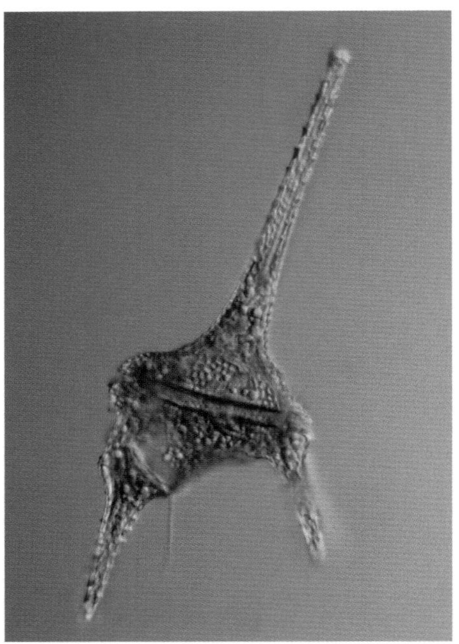

LEFT: *Magnified image (10x) of a freshwater copepod, known commonly as "cyclops" because of its single red eyespot*
MIDDLE: *Magnified image (400x) of heliozoan protozoa*
RIGHT: *Magnified image (25x) of a freshwater dinoflagellate*

Breathe This!

When plant plankton (phytoplankton) use the sun's energy to make their own food (photosynthesis), they release oxygen. There is so much plankton in all the world's oceans that nearly half of Earth's oxygen is produced by these little living things! The next time you take a deep breath, give thanks to those helpful phytoplankton.

The Ups and Downs of Plankton

Plankton get their name from the Greek word meaning "wanderers" or "drifters." But don't think that plankton are pushovers. While they can't control their horizontal movement in the ocean currents, many kinds of plankton can swim vertically, traveling several hundred meters a day. Dinoflagellates [die-noh-FLA-jill-its] are incredibly fast for their size, going up to ten body lengths per second. And a kind of animal plankton known as copepods [koh-puh-pods] can zoom underwater at nearly 14 inches (35 cm) per second. That's like a human swimming the 100-meter freestyle in 5 seconds, in a pool of filled with honey. (Take that, Michael Phelps!) Copepods are not only speedy, they are good for you (assuming you're a fish). Copepods are one of the richest sources of protein in the ocean. These little creatures (whose name means "oar feet," which you can see from the picture) are also found in most freshwater habitats, too.

TRY THIS! *Make a Plankton Net*

While the ocean is filled with plankton, they aren't lumped together in one area. They are spread throughout the salty water. So, if you want to look at a plankton up close, you first need to gather some. You can try shouting, "Come here, little planky-planky." But, sadly, this almost never works. A much smarter strategy is making a homemade plankton net.

What you need

- a pair of nylon stockings (panty hose)
- wire coat hanger
- pair of pliers
- small plastic bottle with a fairly small mouth size (such as an old pill bottle)
- sharp scissors
- stapler or duct tape
- rubber band (a medium wide one works best)
- a washer, a plastic ring, or long tie-tape
- strong string (such as kite string) or fine nylon twine
- small magnifying glass
- dark-colored tray or cookie sheet
- a grownup to help you

How to build it

1. Use scissors to cut off one of the legs of the nylons near the top. Cut a small hole at the toe end about the same size as the mouth opening of your plastic bottle.
2. Carefully unwind the coat hanger and create a ring about 6-10 inches (15-25 cm) in diameter (the right size to fit inside the top of the stocking leg). Use pliers to twist the ends of the hanger together.
3. Put the top end of the stocking leg through the wire ring and fold the nylon back over the outside of the wire ring.
4. Staple or duct tape the nylon leg to the wire ring.
5. Stretch the toe end of the stocking over the mouth of the plastic bottle.
6. Wrap the rubber band tightly around the nylon so it stays attached to the bottle.
7. Cut three pieces of string, each about 2 feet (60 cm) long, and attach them evenly spaced to the coat hanger. Tie the other end of these strings to a washer or plastic ring, and attach this ring to a piece of string.

How to use it

Take your plankton net to a nearby ocean, lake or pond. With an adult helping you, drag the net through the water by hand for a few minutes. The longer you drag your net, the more plankton you'll catch. You can catch even more plankton if you drag your net off the side of a slow moving rowboat, kayak, or canoe. (If you dangle it off a slow-moving motorboat, make sure it is far away from the propeller.)

Back on land, dump the bottle onto a dark-colored tray or cookie sheet. You may see little dots swimming around. That's plankton! Try holding a magnifying glass over your sample to see even smaller plankton. It's important that you don't wait too long. Otherwise, the plankton you caught will die.

A satellite photo of a plankton bloom off the coast of Namibia, in southern Africa

When Plankton Get Together

Individual plankton are quite small, but when they reproduce and grow in large numbers, they can be a startling sight.

In large numbers, plankton have the power to change the color of the water. See the cloudy turquoise blue stuff swirling in this satellite view of the ocean? This plankton party is called a *plankton bloom*. The ocean currents have caused the swirly patterns in the water. When different kinds of plankton create red-colored blooms, it is called *red tides*. Red tides, which are caused by billions and billions of dinoflagellates, can be poisonous to both fish and humans.

Mind-Blowing Fact

Plankton weigh almost nothing—but there are so darn many of them. That's why all the world's plankton population weighs more than the every dolphin, fish, and whale put together!

Even Smaller Than Plankton?!

The ocean is teaming with all sorts of bacteria. Much in the way that astronomers are often finding new stars and planets far off in outer space, microbiologists are discovering new kinds of bacteria. Some scientists even think that there could even be ten million different kinds of bacteria in the ocean.

Bacteria have been found in water where the environment would be too extreme for humans to survive. For example, at the ocean floor, more than 1.3 miles (2 km) below the surface, the water pressure is so intense, we'd be crushed in an instant. Down there the water temperature is just above freezing, but there is super-hot, toxic water gushing out of cracks in the ocean floor. These are called *hydrothermal vents*, nicknamed "black smokers." Some kinds of bacteria call this home. And because bacteria can survive here, so do other deep sea animals that rely on this bacteria for food.

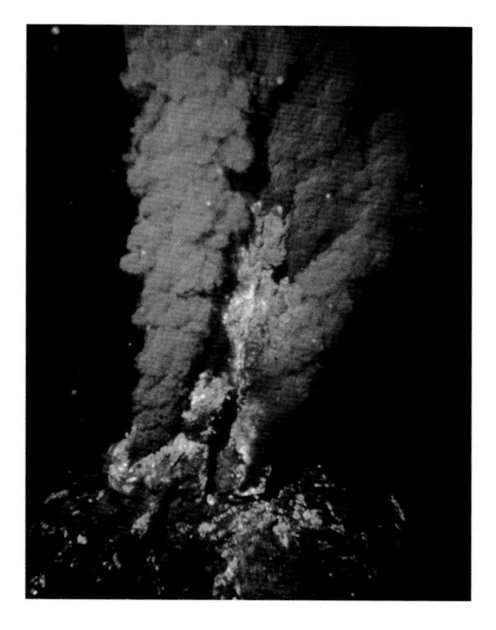

A hydrothermal vent (nicknamed a "black smoker") at the bottom of the Atlantic Ocean

Bioluminescence in Bermuda

Did you know that many ocean animals can glow in the dark? Scientists called this ability *bioluminescence* [Bi-oh-loo-min-NESS-ense]. One tiny glowing animal is the Bermuda fireworm (*Odontosyllis enopla*). Every month, a few days after a full moon, thousands and thousands of tiny female fireworms float to the surface and release a glow-in-the-dark slime. This is how they attract a mate for spawning. It's their way of telling the male fireworms, "Hey, sweet stuff. Come over to my place." Male fireworms go nuts for this glow, and when the males arrive, the females release their eggs, and the males fertilize them.

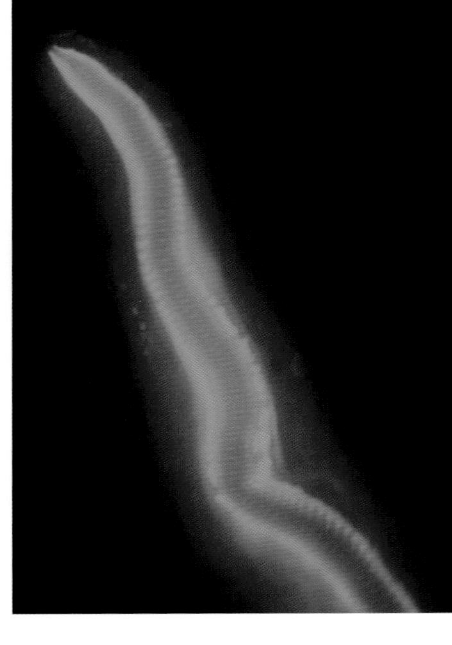

SOME LIKE IT HOT

Most living things would die in the hot springs in Yellowstone National Park. But special heat-loving bacteria called *thermophiles* thrive here. Scientists believe that thermophiles are similar to the first bacteria that lived on Earth, when the planet surface was much hotter. In fact, many of the stunning, bright colors in the springs are produced by bacteria.

At quick glance, Berkley Pit Lake might look like a lovely place to cool off. But once you know the facts, though, you definitely wouldn't put on your swimsuit and dive in. This body of water is totally toxic. If you jumped in, the stinky, poisonous water would burn your eyes, stain your clothes, and injure your skin. If you happen to swallow a mouthful of this lake's water, it would first burn your throat, then poison you. No fish live in this lake, no mosquitoes buzz near it, and there are no plants nearby. In 1995, several hundred migrating snow geese visited this lake for the night. By morning, all were dead.

How did this lake get this way? For over a hundred years, it was part of a large copper mine, where workers pulled tons of copper ore from the ground. When the company shut down in early 1980s, they turned off the pumps that had been keeping out the fresh ground water. What was a 3,900 foot (1.2 km) deep hole filled up with millions of gallons of water that flowed through 10,000 miles of abandoned mine shafts and tunnels. The result was a lake filled with acid water.

You might think that no living thing could survive in this harsh lake. Turns out that this lake is the happy home to many bizarre microscopic creatures. More than a hundred kinds of bacteria, algae, and fungi survive here.

Here's the biggest shock of all! Scientists have discovered that medicines made from some of these bacteria can attack ovarian cancer cells and treat lung tumors. While there is more research to be done, these strange and unusual microbes might pave the way for medical miracles.

OPPOSITE PAGE, TOP: *Berkley Pit Lake, though toxic to humans, is home to countless bacteria, algae, and fungi.*
BELOW: *Bacteria Mat, Yellowstone National Park. Beautiful tapestry of color caused by bacteria that grow in the run-off geyser water*

Lily pond in the late afternoon

SQUIGGLING IN A POND NEAR YOU!

You needn't travel to a toxic pond or the bottom of the ocean to find cool microscopic creatures. Many bizarre microbes live in water much closer to your home. These interesting, invisible organisms can be found in lakes, rivers, ponds, and swamps. That's why it is wise to make sure a body of water is safe before you swim in it. And it's never a good idea to take a sip of water from a lake or pond. Otherwise, you might swallow a bunch of mini-creatures that could make you sick.

On the opposite page are a few of the fascinating creatures that might live in lakes, rivers, and ponds in your area.

Actinastrumhantzii

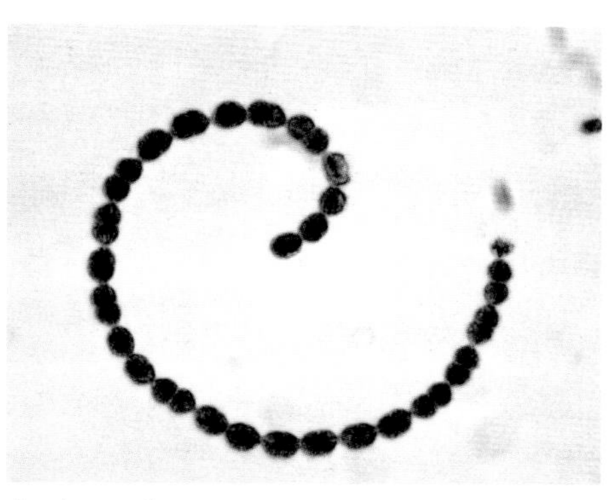

Anabaenaflosaquae

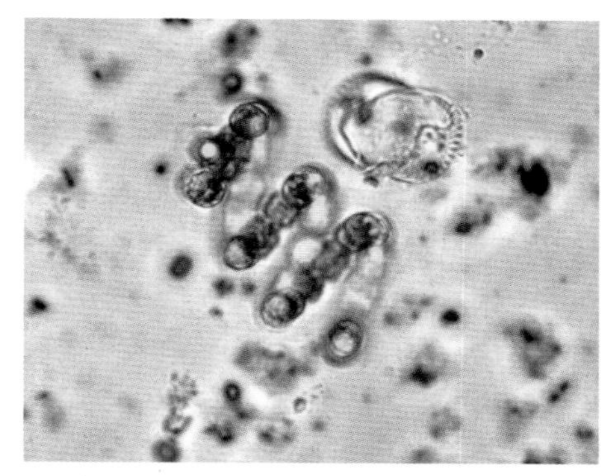

Anabaenaspiroides

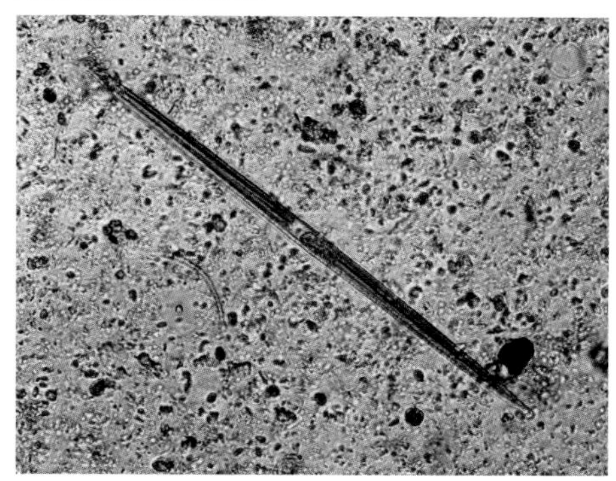

Closterium

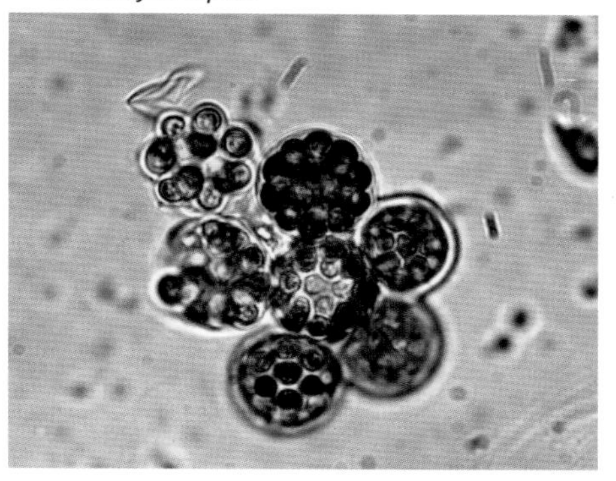

Coelastrummicroporum

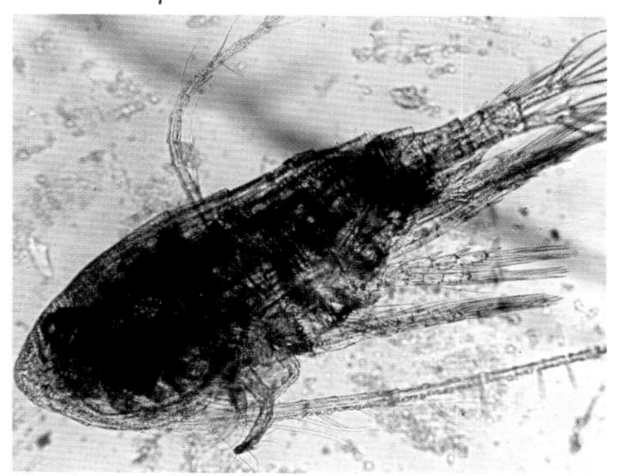

Diaptomus

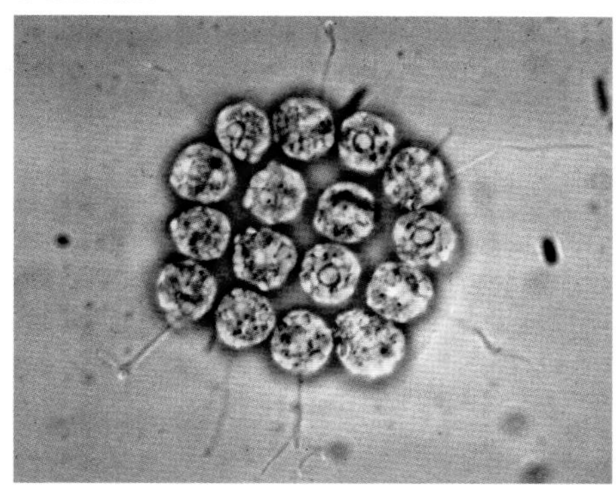

Goniumpectorale

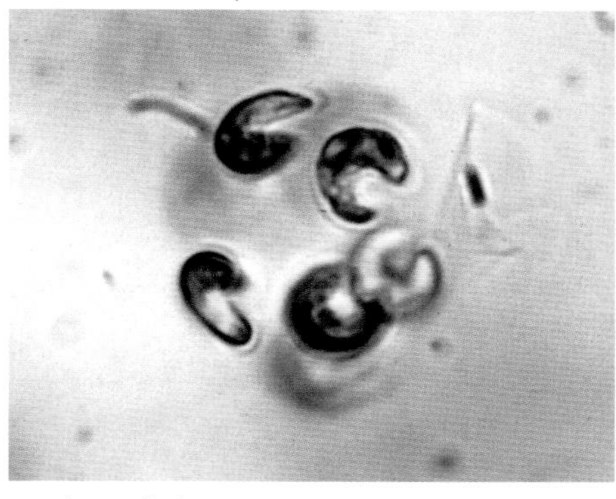

Kirchneriellalunaris

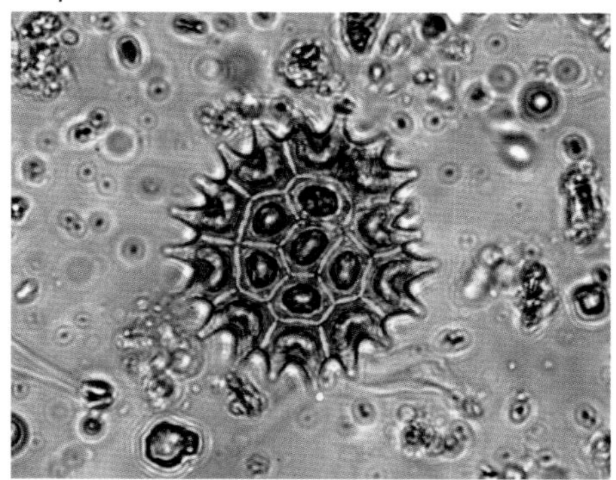

Pediastrumboryanum

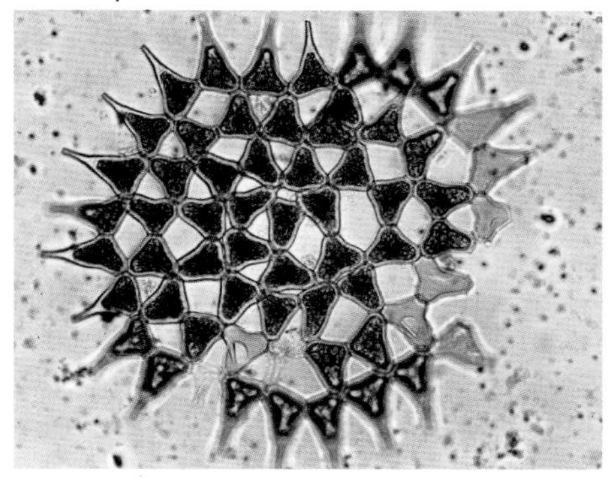

Pediastrumsimplex

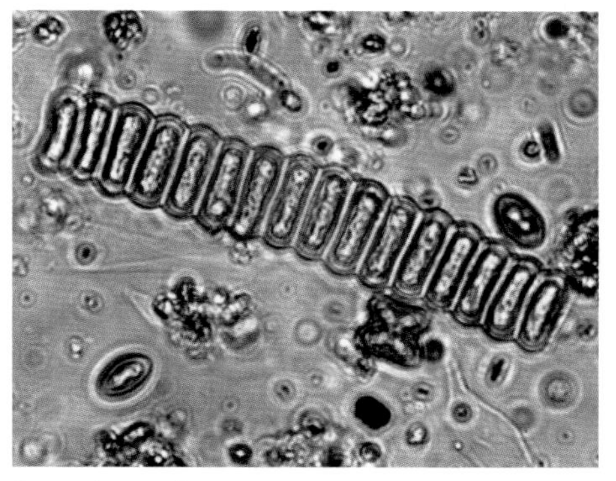

Scenedesmusbijunga

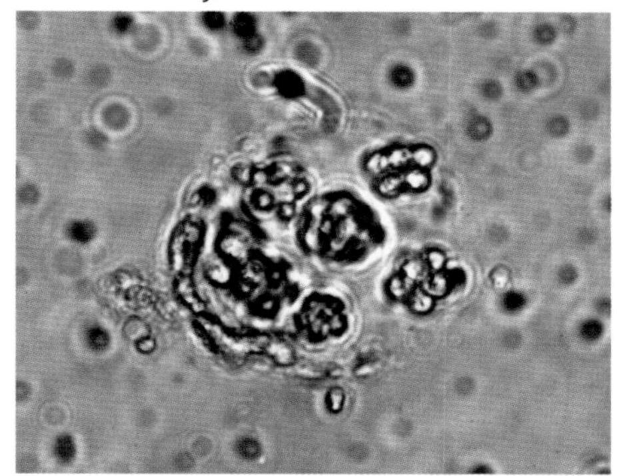

Sphaerocystisschroeteri

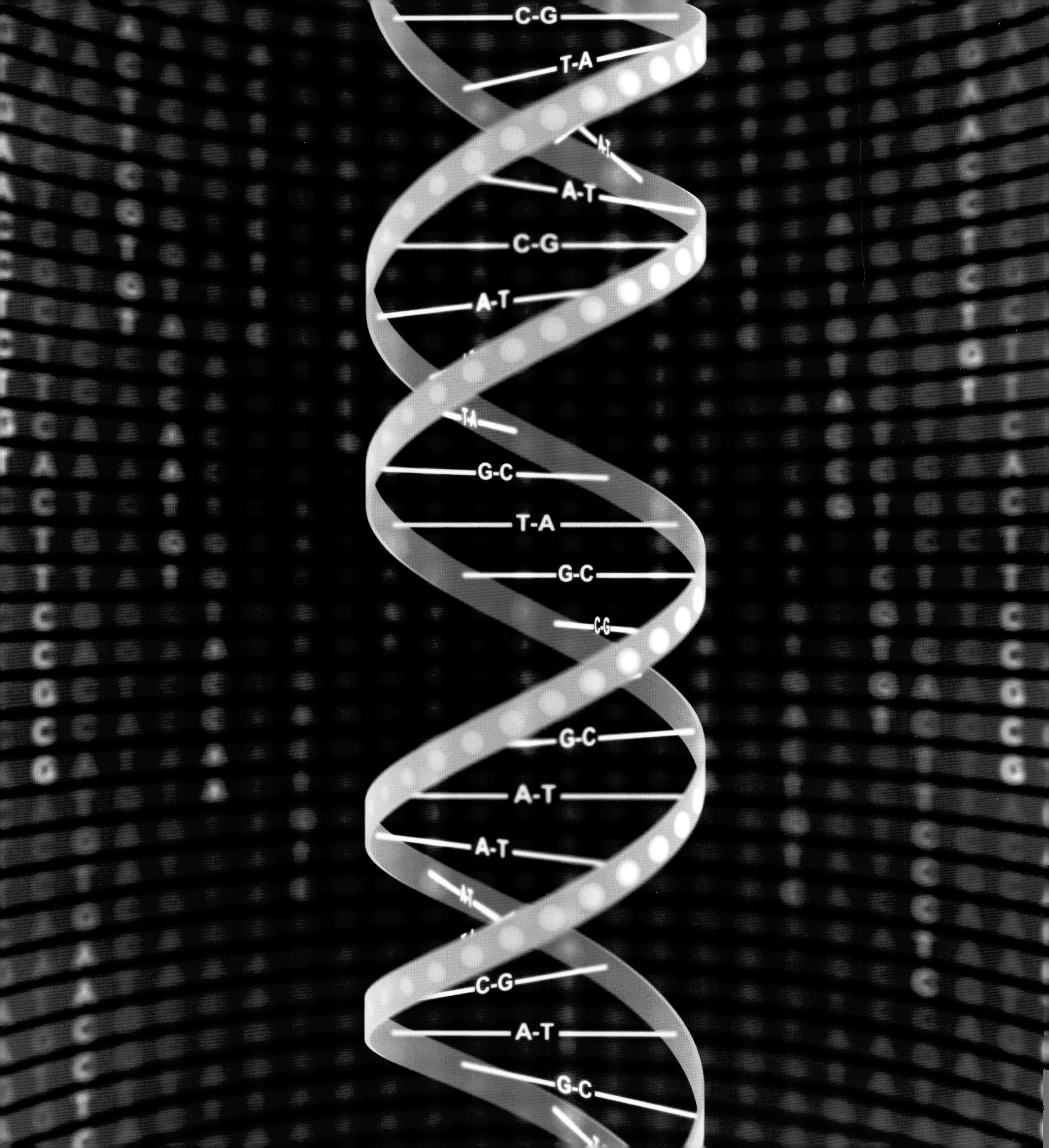
C-G
T-A
A-T
C-G
A-T
G-C
T-A
G-C
G-C
A-T
A-T
C-G
A-T
G-C

CHAPTER

Give My Creature Life!

So far, in this book, you've met a wide variety of tiny creatures, from bedbugs to bacteria. And the search isn't over! Every year, curious scientists discover new species of teeny insects, micro-spiders, and itty-bitty bacteria. So what is the smallest living thing in the whole world? It turns out the answer is "it depends on whom you ask." Huh? Can't scientists use their high-tech micro-tools to simply measure which kind of life is the smallest? Sure, but the problem is agreeing on "what is life?" The question might seem simple, but it's not. Take viruses, for example. These microscopic things are responsible for many diseases including the common cold. But should we consider them living creatures? Many scientists say that viruses are non-living because they cannot survive by themselves—they need to get their energy from the host cells they invade. But other scientists do not agree, arguing that viruses are living things because they contain genetic material like DNA and RNA.

THE INGREDIENTS OF LIFE

Imagine you were hired by a big Hollywood company to create your own microscopic robot for a science-fiction movie. What would your mini-machine need to do in order to convince the world that it was a living creature?

To explore the answer, let's think about the kinds of behaviors that all living things do. First, they can move by themselves from one place to the other. Doesn't matter if they hop, run, slither, or fly; if they can move, they are probably alive. Second, all living animals grow and develop. Take you, for instance. You began life as a single cell in your mother's womb. Soon, this cell split into two; and those cells divided, until eventually you became a human with trillions of cells. Third, all living things are able to reproduce. In order to survive, any species must be able to

OPPOSTITE PAGE: *A computer-generated model of DNA*

make more of itself. Living things pass on traits or features from parent to child. If a girl has red curly hair, there's a good chance others in her family do, too. When a mother tiger gives birth to her young, they are not going to be born donkeys or frogs. The mother passed her DNA onto her young, so that's why they look like her. Lastly, let's not forget, all living things die.

THE WORLD'S SMALLEST ROBOT

As you may have noticed, the latest gadgets and gizmos are smaller than ever. Years ago, it took an entire room to hold a computer. These days, many computers can fit in the palm of your hand. The same goes with robots.

A few years ago, a team of scientists at Dartmouth University invented a super-small micro-robot. It is so small that 200 of these robots could fit on a plain M&M. It is so little that it could easily play hide-and-seek on Abraham Lincoln's beard on a U.S. penny!

The micro-robot is about as wide as a human hair (60 micrometers).

Computer-generated model of what microscopic machines called "nanobots" might look like in the bloodstream

Bruce Donald, the head scientist on this project, explained that this micro-robot is controllable like a car. "You can steer it anywhere on a flat surface." This robot doesn't move in a pre-set pattern. Its movements are based on electrical changes in the silicon grid it moves on. These charges also give this robot its power. And it is fast and nimble, moving in different directions quite quickly. This micro-robot can move two millimeters every second. While this might not seem like much, keep in mind that for these tiny guys, that is a huge distance. It's like a human running 50 miles (about 80 kilometers) per hour!

In the past, most micro-robots had tiny wheels or joints that caused the robots to stick to every surface they traveled on. To fix this problem, the scientists made this micro-robot move

"Water bears" in space!

It doesn't take much to kill most kinds of living things on Earth. Cut out food and water, and any creature will eventually die. If you expose the living thing to extreme heat or cold, radiation, or intense pressure, its end comes almost instantly. That's why scientists were surprised that almost invisible roly-poly creatures called *tardigrades* survived recent trips to outer space.

Normally, tardigrades (nicknamed "water bears") live in lakes and oceans and among plants like mosses and lichens. But scientists deprived some "lucky" tardigrades of food and water for years, zapped them with radiation, and put them in temperatures as hot as 311°F (155°C) and as cold as -300°F (-200°C). These microbes were even sent out into orbit for ten days—and still these species survived!

Real "water bears" (tardigrades) aren't this colorful. This image has been colored to highlight its details.

like a little caterpillar, making incredibly small hops: 20,000 per second! According to Donald, "It turns by putting a silicon 'foot' out and pivoting like a motorcyclist skidding around a tight turn."

With all the countless forms of little life on the planet, what would be the point of inventing a micro-machine? The inventors of this technology say that one day these micro-robots could explore dangerous environments, might be able to help repair or change human cells, and could even protect information in a computer system.

CHAPTER

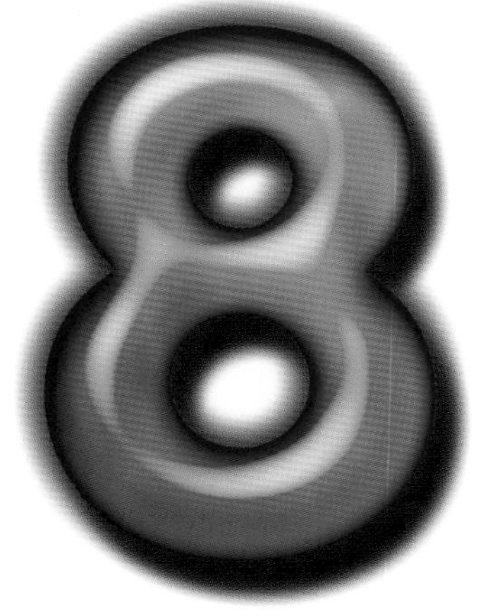

Learning to Love "the Little Guys"

Has this book turned you into an enthusiastic micro-maniac? Or are you now even more terrified of germs and tiny bugs?

It's not easy to appreciate the countless creepy little creatures that live in, on, and all around us. After all, many types of bacteria and viruses can, in fact, make us quite sick—that is when they're not busy killing us. As for tiny blood-sucking critters like ticks and bedbugs, no one would put them on their "cutest living creature" list.

Before you wish that the world were rid of these little living things, remember all the good things that these hearty little guys do for us. Many kinds of microbes help by fighting off the harmful varieties. And, thanks to microbes, humans have been able to create tasty foods like bread, cheese, chocolate, and more. While you might get annoyed with some mold or fungus that make some food gross and inedible, without these little creatures digesting the world around them, our world would be overflowing with dead plants and bodies.

Some folks fool themselves into thinking that humans are—and always have been—the dominant lifeform on the planet. Hah! For starters, people have been on Earth for about 200,000 years. This might sound like a long time, but it's a mere blip compared to how long some microscopic species that have been around. The first known bacteria appeared a few *billion* years before that. And, chances are, some types of bacteria will probably survive on our planet long, long after humans become extinct. Without the earliest microbes, there would probably be no "us" at all. Fossil evidence suggests that your great-great-great-great-great . . . (keep going for a billion "greats") grandparent was a bacterium.

When Anton van Leeuwenhoek became the first person to see microbes back in the 1600s, he discovered a whole new world

squirming and squiggling with fascinating little creatures. Since then, scientists have developed super-powerful microscopes that give us close-up views of remarkable life that was once invisible.

You've got to hand it to the "little guys" that live among us. They are incredibly pervasive, adaptive, and resilient (not that a protozoan could appreciate the compliment).

Before things get out of hand, remember to wash yours as often as possible. I'll end with a special shout-out to the little silverfish who might be nibbling on the pages of this very book some day in a dusty library or bookstore. BACK OFF!

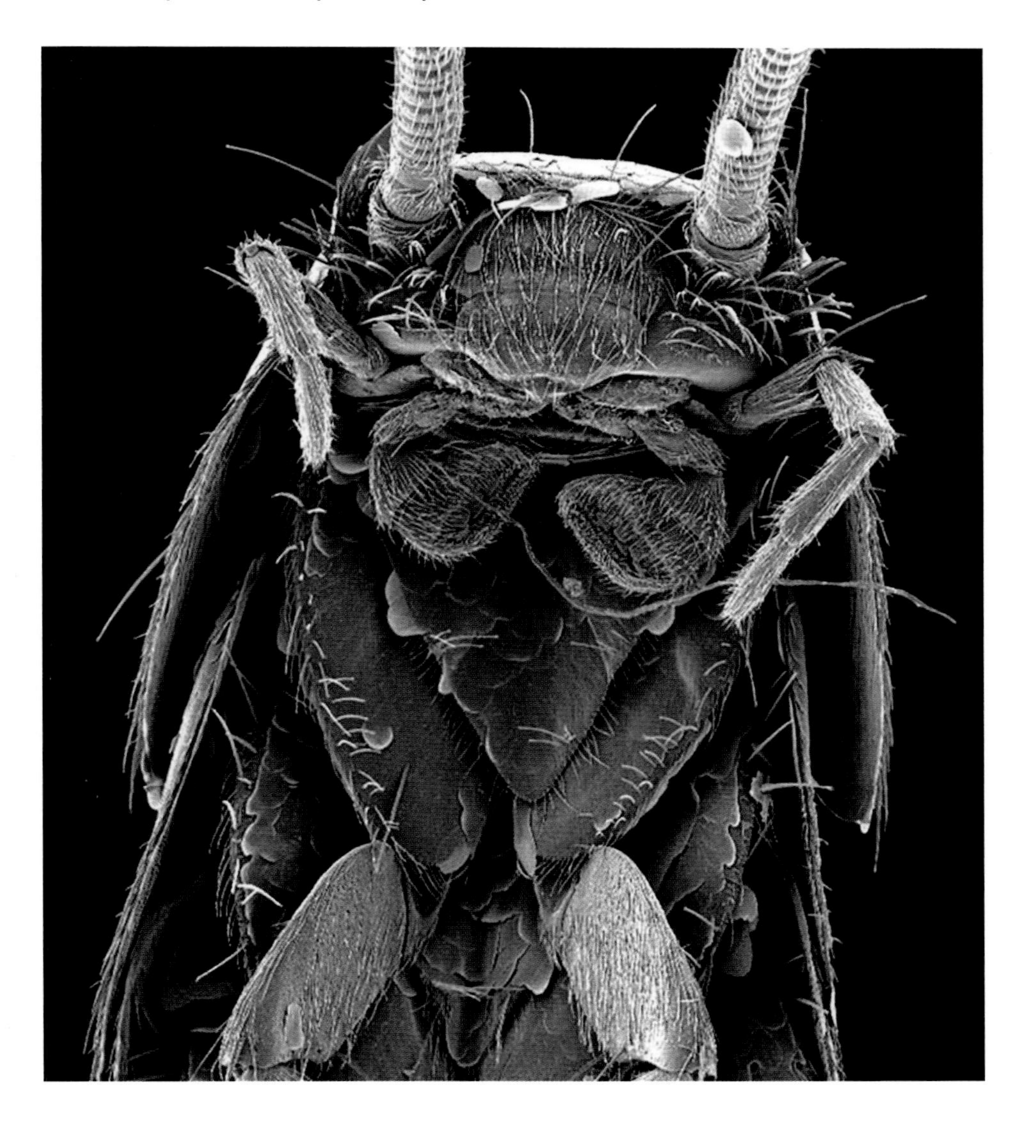

OPPOSITE PAGE: *Billions of years ago, when much of Earth was covered with volcanoes, boulder-like stromatolites formed. These fossils were caused by the pileup of microscopic blue-green algae (cyanobacteria) over thousands of years. Stromatolites still exist on Earth today.*
LEFT: *Silverfish have been crawling the planet long before the first humans . . . and will probably be here long after humans become extinct.*